Lessons From the Landscape

My path to business success and personal fulfillment

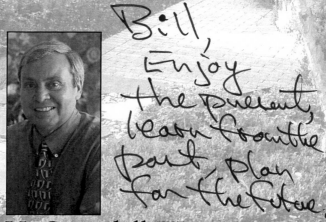

*Bill,
Enjoy the present, learn from the past, plan for the future,

Frank Crandall*

Frank H. Crandall III

Wood River Productions

Published by Wood River Productions
101 Woodville Road, Hope Valley, RI 02832

Crandall, Frank H. III.
    Lessons from the landscape: My path to business success and personal fulfillment : Frank H. Crandall III – Hope Valley, RI: Wood River Productions

    ISBN 0-9773011-0-9

1. Success in business. 2. Motivation. 3. Self-help.

Cover and book design by Ken Mazur,
Microcomputer/Editorial Consultants

Project coordination and marketing by Lynda Martel,
Alternative Marketing

Picture Credits: Roland Gutierrez, Shane Photography,
                            Warwick, R.I., Pgs. 77, Back Cover
                            John Hames, Pg. 87
                            Ken Mazur, Pgs. 71, 130
                            Frank Crandall, all other photos

Printed in the United States of America
By Reynolds DeWalt of New Bedford, Mass.

DEDICATION

Because of the lasting influence they have had on my life, because of their guidance and support as I made my own way, and because of their constant love ... I dedicate this book to my parents, Frank and Betty Crandall.

ACKNOWLEDGEMENTS

It takes many people to make a book happen. Getting thoughts organized and written down on paper is only the beginning of a long process—one that I could not have accomplished without the help of two people in particular:

Lynda Martel, who owns Alternative Marketing, guided the initial editing process, organized the story content, and transcribed my handwritten notes. She also researched publication options and promoted the book locally and regionally.

Ken Mazur, Wood River Evergreens' valuable and steadfast systems manager and president of Microcomputer / Editorial Consultants, performed the massive roles of editing, graphic design, pre-print production, and all-around creative influence.

Ken and Lynda always supported the needs of this project and were a constant source of motivation as we worked together as a team. I am blessed to be in partnership with these two dedicated and talented business people whom I can also call my friends. Without them this publication might not have been possible.

TABLE OF CONTENTS

INTRODUCTION

Like many people, I have always wanted to write a book and record the highlights and events of my life. In the fall of 2004 I not only had the time but the motivation to actually sit down and get it done.

Teaching has always been a passion of mine. First it was biology. Later it became landscaping. And from 2001 to 2003, I ran a series of GEM business seminars with Lynda Martel and Ken Mazur. The seminars were designed to provide useful business information to progressive-thinking Green Industry trades people so they could improve and grow their own businesses. Many attendees wanted me to expand on some of the seminar topics further.

That request planted the seed of a book idea, which was fertilized by the timing of a powerful transformation I had undergone on both a personal and business level. I had a compelling story to tell. I needed to share it so that I could teach others about pitfalls they might encounter and how to avoid them.

I don't pretend to know all the answers. I can only speak about what happened to me, how I responded, and the results. I do know that by sharing the valuable lessons I learned on my journey through life as a business owner, husband, and human being, I might help others avoid some of the mistakes I made.

If only one person is better informed after reading this book, the task of writing it will have been worthwhile.

CHAPTER 1
REFLECTING ON THE JOURNEY

"The purpose of life is not to win. The purpose of life is to grow and share.
When you come to look back on all that you have done in life, you will get
more satisfaction from the pleasure you have brought to other people's lives
than you will from the times that you outdid and defeated them."

Rabbi Harold Kushner

Recently, I was planting and pruning in the gardens of Wood River Evergreens' (WRE) Landscape Design Showcase in preparation for a fundraising event to benefit the Master Gardener Foundation of Rhode Island, Inc.

Looking up from my work, I took in with delight the lush gardens and inviting stone paths that wound their way around many brilliant flowers and the sparkling waterfall and streams that occupied the landscape around me. What an extraordinary transformation this land had undergone since our Christmas retail shop was destroyed by fire 3 1/2 years ago! With optimism, lots of hard work, and a plan, our talented team had rebuilt the charred structure, and its fresh appearance inspired us to upgrade all our other buildings and install these beautiful themed gardens.

Moving to a stone bench in the Japanese garden, thoughts darted through my mind like the colorful Koi fish under the lotus leaves shading the fishpond. This property was not the only thing that had transformed over the past few years. So had my business—and so had I.

I reflected on how my business had started as compared to what it looked like today. The vision I had embraced years ago has been realized. I enjoy my current roles as salesperson, speaker and company visionary, and I work with a team of professionals I thoroughly enjoy. My chosen profession is in alignment with my personal passions and I am surrounded by natural beauty every day. My personal transformation through the years has left me feeling content, relaxed, and happy. There were many things I had to let go of—not always an easy task—to realize this new me, but in retrospect it was the only choice I had to get from there to here. I am truly blessed.

Like the gardens around me, everything in my life has changed, which is probably the most important lesson I learned on my journey to here and now. There were seasons of abundance, and seasons of scarcity. As one thing expired another sprang forth with new life. Change is the natural order of the landscape; it is the natural order of life. It is impossible to stop and impossible to control. "Letting go" is the only sane solution.

Letting go. I had to let go of so many things to reach this point, yet I feel more fulfilled than ever before. At first daunting, letting go has become liberating and rewarding beyond my wildest dreams! Letting go on the business side has meant delegating responsibilities to key team managers, and this has transformed our business into a more professional, more efficient operation. Tasks that used to take me hours, now take only minutes. Relinquishing control of the budget to my accounting manager took years to put into practice, but is now routine as she keeps track of our financial expenditures to ensure our continued success.

I let go of my fear of technology and now do everything on a computer, from sending daily emails and creating estimates in Excel®, to downloading digital files of worksites. I do sales presentations with greater efficiency and speed. I sketch out landscape design ideas on digital photos that I download onto my laptop, re-size in PhotoShop®, and print out in black and white. When I meet with a client to review ideas these visual elements typically help me finalize a contract that day. It is not unusual to finalize several spring projects in this way, some generating over $175,000 in sales value.

The work environment here has changed as well. Letting go of an early (and uncomfortable) leadership style resulted in many new, positive management procedures. As I became more focused and calm—a "serving" leader, centered in the present, clear about my vision, and happy—the company became a better place to work at as a result.

Delegating responsibilities to my staff resulted in surprising and beneficial transformations among them as well. After suggesting that maintenance and construction managers meet to improve our job reporting forms and discuss equipment, vehicle and personnel needs for the spring, they responded with detailed reports outlining our seasonal equipment and vehicle needs as well as their related costs, a list of personnel needs and interviews they had scheduled with prospective candidates. They also presented several job reporting forms incorporating recommended improvements. What a huge step forward! My managers now take full responsibility for the process and tools that help their jobs go better. This is a long way from the resistance I experienced earlier when first attempting to give managers new responsibilities.

At a recent WRE winter planning meeting, I outlined my vision for the company over the next three to five years, which involves the transformation of WRE into a truly "Green" business by adopting environmentally friendly or organic landscape planting, maintenance and lawn-care practices for our clients' properties as well as for our nursery and greenhouse operations. The response from the WRE team was overwhelmingly supportive. Many asked to take the Northeast Organic Farming Association (NOFA) accreditation course in organic land care as soon as it could be scheduled. This too is a dramatic change from the resistance my new ideas once met. WRE has grown and transformed into a different company from the initial vision of a landscape firm I had in 1972. It will continue to grow and evolve over time as we continue to embrace change and move forward.

When I was growing up, I always strived for perfection and when things didn't go exactly the way I envisioned I would get frustrated, anxious, and sometimes angry. The combination of my personal shortcomings, trying to do everything on the job myself, becoming overwhelmed with no way out, and feeling frustrated and angry, left me depressed and turned me into a workaholic. I had no time or energy left for my own self.

That has all changed over the last three years and the lessons I've learned are central to the writing of this book. Moving from an owner-dominated business to a participatory-managed company was not easy. Neither were the personal changes I faced nor the personal losses I experienced. Now I realize my goal is to strive for excellence with the understanding that mistakes and failures may occur, but each time I delegate more responsibilities the teams perform their jobs better, more efficiently and more professionally than I would be able to do.

Resuming my work in the gardens I reflected once more on the winding paths—those that led to my business success and personal fulfillment. As humbling and painful as the journey was, it was the perfect journey for me. And I am quite happy to share the lessons I learned from the setbacks and successes along the way.

Lessons from the landscape indeed.

How did my company and I make the passage? First we had to step onto the path.

Wood River Evergreens' Landscape Design Showcase features paver patios, walkways and a variety of gardens.

CHAPTER 2

STEPPING ONTO THE PATH

"History will be kind to me for I intend to write it."

Winston Churchill

A Modest Beginning: 1968- 1984

In the summer of 1968 I began my own landscaping business after mowing lawns for other companies. Although I mowed lawns most of the time, I also learned to prune shrubs, weed and mulch garden beds, install new plants, and perform miscellaneous tasks to open or close my clients' summer homes each season.

After graduating from Westerly High School in 1970, I entered the University of Rhode Island (URI) and majored in botany, education, political science and history. Throughout my years at URI, I continued to maintain 35 properties in Weekapaug, R.I., working after classes each day and on the weekends. The money I made landscaping (along with several scholarships) paid for my undergraduate education.

At the completion of my sophomore year in 1972, I married Penny Bader, moved into one of her parents' rental homes, and founded Wood River Evergreens. Our modest beginning consisted of planting 2,000 white spruce seedlings in an abandoned 4-acre field. My plan was to raise Christmas trees and continue landscaping part-time while earning my bachelor's degree.

I graduated from URI in 1974, but, unable to gain entry into law school, I returned for an additional year while dabbling in landscaping full-time in the summers of 1974 and 1975. By the end of 1975 I obtained my teaching certificate for grades 7 through 12 in the sciences and history and accepted teaching and coaching positions at Killingly High School in Danielson, Conn. where I taught biology and coached cross-country and indoor and outdoor track from 1975 to 1984.

During those nine years our Christmas tree business grew substantially from its opening in 1978. By 1984 we were selling 600 trees a season, making 300 to 400 wreaths, and running free hayrides with Santa around the fields on our property.

I worked hard to make our cut-tree services unique. We shook each tree free of debris, drilled a hole in the trunk for mounting in the stand, wrapped each tree in netting for easier handling, installed some of the trees in a patented 4-brace tree stand, and delivered many trees to clients' homes—all for free.

During my teaching and coaching years, I also maintained several properties but began to transition into the landscape construction end of the business. I planted new trees and shrubs, re-mulched beds, did more pruning, and even began installing brick walkways. Occasionally I harbored thoughts of making a full-time effort in the landscaping business, but at the end of each summer I returned to teaching and coaching with enthusiasm—until 1984.

By that time I had a master's degree and 30 credits towards a Certificate of Advanced Graduate Studies at Rhode Island College, but I was only earning $17,000 as a teacher plus $3,000 as a coach. Frustrated with my meager earnings, I decided I would leave teaching at the end of the school year to start landscaping full time. To be sure I was making a wise choice, I first took an 8-week course with a career counselor at Options, Inc. in Providence, R.I. At the end of the course, my counselor announced that I should be running my own business, something I had wanted to do for a long time.

Frank's 1972 GMC pickup hauling woodchips to a project in Weekapaug, R.I.

Although my wife Penny was aware that I was frustrated with my teaching salary, she didn't realize I was seriously considering a career change until June of 1984 when I told her that I hadn't renewed my contract and that we would be entering the landscape and Christmas business full time. This was a critical mistake I would later regret because my decision resulted in unexpected financial setbacks that dramatically changed our lifestyle. With advanced notice, discussion and planning as a couple, these changes might have been avoided, or at least could have been handled differently.

Fulfilling A Dream: 1985-1989

For better (or worse), I fulfilled a dream to run my own landscaping business. I had no business plan, no financial projections and no budget; I had only a passion for landscaping, a strong work ethic and a desire to make this career move a success. No wonder Penny was concerned!

The frustrations, economic hardships and suffering my family ultimately endured as a result of my new business venture could have been alleviated with a thorough, well-thought-out business plan. Unfortunately, that revelation would not take place until 1992 when we were on the verge of bankruptcy. Initially, however, the economy was strong enough for our landscaping and Christmas business to grow and prosper. The first year of full-time effort generated $50,000 in gross sales, enough for me to continue business operations the next year, although it was still not nearly enough revenue for me to take a regular pay.

Penny and I were expecting our third child that year and she was forced to abandon her career in banking to be a stay-at-home mom. Although our three children—Frank IV (8 years old), Jason (3 years old) and our newborn, Heather—benefited greatly from her daily care, the burden of supporting our family fell solely upon my fledgling business. Not an easy task!

Each year, from 1986 to 1989, the landscape projects we did became more complex and high-end, requiring new trucks, tractors, equipment and personnel. Gross sales were increasing dramatically

1988 Family photo taken during the December Christmas season: (from left) Penny, Heather, Frank IV, Jason and Frank III.

each year and by 1989 our sales totaled over $900,000. WRE was on its way to becoming a million dollar company!

Our Christmas tree business expanded as well. In 1989 we were earning gross sales of over $115,000. But even with this tremendous increase in business, I still hadn't developed an effective budget program or implemented estimating or job-costing programs. This would prove to be a near-fatal mistake on my part.

In 1990 and 1991, the economy went into a deep recession and our gross sales dropped 50 percent to $450,000. With no contingency plan, the next five years were difficult, emotional, and extremely stressful for Penny, our children, WRE employees and me.

Gaining Wisdom: 1990-1994

To say the early 1990s were learning years is a considerable understatement. Faced with a 50 percent drop in sales, and no plan (or clue), I laid off employees, sold vehicles and equipment, sought loans to pay off debts (including the IRS), and requested re-financing from my banker.

Unfortunately, these steps were not enough. The bank refused to lend us more money and without a very generous loan from my aunt, parents and in-laws, WRE would have ceased to exist.

A course on creating business plans effectively changed our plight, however, and it was my business plan that convinced my banker to refinance our debt and extend us a line of credit, which allowed us to continue business operations and move forward.

Always looking for ways to make additional money by bringing new clients to our nursery and Christmas business, we experimented with agri-entertainment events like The Spooky Halloween Hayride (1991-2000), The Festival of Lights Hayride (1992-1995), and a summer event called The Western Hayride Show (1994).

The Halloween hayride proved to be a very successful event. It attracted thousands of customers to WRE each season, generated much-needed revenue, and gave us an opportunity to cross-market our landscape and Christmas services at the same time. By the year 2000 there were more hayrides competing for the same local consumers, the possibility of liability had risen, and basically all of our employees (including me) were worn out. It was clear the hayride had run its course. We ended the popular Halloween event to devote our energies to our landscaping business, which was not only growing in size but generating bigger profit margins as well.

Growing And Expanding: 1995-2000

With a plan in place, WRE slowly started to recover and grow. By

1995, we had hired 12 employees, owned seven vehicles, and generated gross sales of over $1 million dollars. By 2000, our staff had increased to over 20. We had four business divisions, and 12 trucks and loaders.

This growth and expansion period required new types of changes. We expanded our office and design space, and invested in computers to support our inventory program, customer newsletters, bookkeeping and email. In 1996, we created a website (www.woodriverevergreens.com), one of the first in the horticultural industry. Customer demands motivated us to add more services such as landscape lighting, custom carpentry, landscape design and masonry. Our business had developed a brand name recognized throughout southern New England for high quality, service, integrity, and an exclusive warranty.

The Rhode Island Nursery and Landscape Association (RINLA), which presented us with over 17 landscape excellence awards by the year 2005, also recognized the quality of our services and products.

By 2000 we had become a $2 million company. Landscaping products and services made up over 90 percent of our gross sales.

Tragedy Leads To Triumph: 2000-Present

In February of 2001 a fire destroyed our 2-story Christmas shop building and its contents. My brother Doug, father Frank, father-in-law Ray, and I built the shop in 1986. To see this family landmark destroyed by flames was traumatic but this dark cloud really did have a silver lining.

The tragedy of the fire gave us the opportunity to redesign the shop's interior layout to better serve our needs. We built a conference room and new office space for our designers upstairs, and a salesroom downstairs where we could meet with clients. The facility immediately became more useful, safer, more comfortable and more professional looking.

The process of rebuilding also allowed me to implement a lifetime dream of creating a landscape showcase for our clients. Our landscape designer, Jenn Judge, drew up the plans and our staff eventually installed the showcase over a two-year period. The WRE Landscape Design Showcase features a wide variety of themed gardens and design elements such as landscape lighting, water features, custom carpentry, stonework and a sound system. It is the only one of its kind in southern New England.

Since the year 2000, WRE has developed into a stronger company. We now have a staff of 35, gross sales between $2.5 and $3 million, and a fleet of 17 vehicles. Our operations are guided by detailed business and marketing plans, a comprehensive budget, and a sophisticated computer system. I delegate many more responsibilities to team members. Our landscape projects are still primarily residential with 75 percent of sales generated from construction and 25 percent from maintenance. We have also acquired a number of commercial accounts which now represent five percent of sales.

Much has changed since the dark days of the early 1990s. Our business experience has resulted in a more professional company, and my own personal growth has helped me become a better leader.

CHAPTER 3
LEAD WITH A VISION

"Visions are the vehicles that transport us across the boundaries of current reality to the boundless hopes of a future seemingly beyond our grasp. What once we deemed impossible, becomes not only possible but probable when we live out our vision through actions."

Gerald Michaelson (Sun Tzu)

Where do you want to be in five years? Ten years? Where do you want your business to be in the future? These are important questions to consider as you plan out your personal and business "grand strategy"—in other words, your vision of the future.

As the visionary in my company, I am continually expanding, refining and articulating WRE's grand strategy for the future; the details of our current and future plans are updated regularly in our five-year business plan. It is amazing to watch our vision become reality once it has been written, clearly explained and shared with the entire team.

Although I have always had a vision of building a one-stop, award-winning, multimillion-dollar coastal landscape-design construction and maintenance firm, serious progress towards that goal didn't begin until I formed a planning committee with several key employees, clearly explained my goals to them and solicited their support.

I learned this lesson the hard way: You must bring participants into a process. They have to understand, embrace and own the goals and strategies so their efforts will be focused, supportive and successful.

In the mid-1990s, as the business began to grow and expand, I was often frustrated by the lack of support I got from key personnel when it came to decisions I was making about adding vehicles, personnel, or equipment that I believed we needed in order to offer additional services. My problem wasn't with my personnel but rather that I had failed to communicate my vision—no wonder they weren't on board!

After several years of disjointed efforts in trying to move the company forward, I shared my vision of where I expected to be in three to five years with my managers and team leaders. When I later requested input from my planning committee my vision quickly became a reality. In fact, several changes in our strategies, as suggested by the planning committee, refined our process and expedited our progress toward our goals.

Being open to changing your strategies is key to achieving the results you desire, especially as economic conditions, competition and financial or personnel resources change.

Using Vision To Effect Change

A skillful leader knows how and when to make adjustments to ensure that goals are achieved. I learned this as a quarterback at Westerly High School. In one game our team used two swift running backs to run sweeps around the opposition team's ends. This worked well in the first half, but their defense made adjustments to stop our sweeps in the second half. Recognizing that the defense was loading up on the outside, I called a change of play to run up the middle, which provided running room for us to march down the field and score the winning touchdown.

Setting a vision with specific goals can change an existing situation. From 1975 through 1984, I took over the position of head coach for the Killingly High School track team. My first year of coaching I had the team set a goal of winning an Eastern Connecticut Conference championship within three years, and a long-term goal of capturing a state championship—which they had not won since 1952. The previous coach had announced to this team that because they hadn't won a conference title in years, they wouldn't again this year. By the time I left Killingly in 1984, the track team had won four outdoor track ECC championships, three indoor track ECC championships, the Class L State Track title in 1983, and runner-up in 1984.

These feats could not have been accomplished without the dedication, talent and focus of all team members and the support of the community. But if you think you are defeated, you are. When I announced to my new team my vision of winning a title, we set that as a common goal we could all work toward.

It worked!

Your business success can be limited by your vision. If you set out to have 50 lawns to maintain with no plans to expand, your business will stay at 50 lawns. If you have a clear vision to create a multidivisional company with two locations servicing primarily commercial accounts, ultimately you will achieve that goal. As the company visionary you must set your sights high and be willing to adjust your strategies as conditions change.

Equally important is creating a personal vision: Where do I want to be in five years and how am I going to get there?

Primarily I planned to create a profitable, comprehensive, landscape company where I would serve in the roles of visionary, client sales, budgeting, marketing, employee training and evaluations; day-to-day operations would be handled by my operations manager. I also wanted to travel to gardens all over the world, become an accomplished photographer, speak at horticultural events, conferences and workshops, and write books on the horticultural business and landscaping. (I always set my goals high, and enjoy the process of working to achieve them.) Since articulating those goals on paper, I have achieved them one by one.

An overriding goal of mine is to make a fundamental difference in people's lives. My life has been so blessed that I feel it is important to "give back" through speaking, writing, my company's services or personal contacts.

What is WRE's vision for the future? In the next three to five years, WRE will be transformed into an organic, environmentally friendly company and will become the leader in these practices in southern New England. It will be an exciting journey as we move to the leading edge of the organic landscape movement and truly become a "Green" company.

LESSONS LEARNED:

1. As the company visionary, set your sights high and be willing to adjust your strategies as conditions change.
2. Bring employees into your planning so they can understand, embrace and own the goals and strategies.

CHAPTER 4

BE FOCUSED, CONFIDENT, PERSISTENT

"The price of success is hard work, dedication to the job at hand, and the determination that whether we win or lose, we have applied the best of ourselves to the task at hand."

Vince Lombardi

Focus

Once a business owner has a clear, defined vision in place, it's important to focus, exude confidence and persist in moving the company toward that vision. Fortunately, as WRE grew, I learned how to focus on critical aspects of running the company and concentrate on what I do best.

Without making changes in both my business operations and my personal life, I would not have found time to write this book. In order to focus on my writing, I eliminated television from my house and organized each day so that I was able to read, research and write for at least three to five hours. As I completed each chapter, I rewarded myself with a dinner out or a trip to Barnes & Nobles to buy more books. With the book 90 percent finished, I decided to write the last chapters in Key West, Fla. at a beautiful resort. (It's interesting how productive we can be when there is a reward to motivate us.)

One of the best books I've read regarding focus, confidence and success is *"The Power of Focus"* by Jack Canfield, Mark Victor-Hansen and Les Hewitt. They identify strategies to help the reader focus on strengths, eliminate what's holding him back, change bad habits, and create a healthy balance between work and family life. This book was invaluable to me as I made the transition from a stressed, controlling, workaholic business owner to a focused, calm owner who delegates responsibilities so he can have a personal life with time for exercise, family and fun.

One quote in the book expresses the importance of having self-confidence: "Experience tells you what to do. Confidence allows you to do it."

Confidence

Most of us know that self-confidence is crucial to achieving goals, taking risks, and overcoming hurdles. It also takes a strong, confident leader to take responsibility for mistakes, sincerely apologize when necessary and move on a revised course to achieve success.

One day, after a frenzied morning meeting and several complaint phone calls, I got into a shouting match with one of my managers who was upset that I had changed the day's work schedule. Our angry exchange carried outside the office to crew members who were getting ready to head out to their daily projects. It was unprofessional of me to blow up at an employee in front of the work crew and office staff, and it was humiliating to the employee. After calming down, I apologized to the employee and we set up guidelines for us to have a productive exchange of ideas and opinions on a regular basis without angry outbursts. The next morning, I also apologized to each member of the crew for my outburst, vowed to seek professional help, and promised to act in a more professional manner in the future.

With counseling, exercise and meditation, I have been able to keep my word. I now deal with stressful situations in a calm, professional way.

As important as your own self-confidence is, instilling confidence in employees and managers is equally critical. Your positive leadership abilities will help to motivate your teammates, build their self-esteem and empower them.

You can empower your managers by clearly defining their tasks, goals and authority, then stepping out of the way to let them accomplish the goals. Give them the freedom to succeed (or sometimes fail). When managers fall short, discuss the reasons why and give them the support and training they need to succeed.

Building confidence can help employees overcome fear of failure, which is essential if they are to move forward. We all make mistakes and fail, but true winners learn from their failures and move on with a renewed determination to succeed.

It also takes confidence to close a deal on a "cold call." In all such cases I find it best to devise a win/win strategy that ensures both parties feel good about the results.

Recently I met with the owners of W. B. Cody's Restaurant in Westerly, R.I. to discuss revisions they wanted to make to their landscape. Cody's is a popular restaurant in a highly visible location frequented by many of my coastal landscape clients. The restaurant is a favorite eating place of mine and I had been surveying the 13-year-old landscape with ideas on ways to dress up the outer grounds to make them more inviting, colorful and professional looking.

I discussed my ideas of transplanting large, overgrown shrubs, dressing up the front roadside sign with a bed of colorful seasonal changeovers, adding a water fountain with lighting, placing planters and flower pots along the entrance, installing a brick paver walkway, and creating planting beds with perennials and flowering shrubs in the landscape. Both Marty and Annie Fox, the owners, enthusiastically approved of the much overdue facelift. I predicted these changes would create a buzz in the community and give the owners a feeling of great satisfaction as the restaurant's outside appearance improved. Recognizing that this highly visible commercial property would provide a great opportunity to promote my company's products and services, I offered the owners a discount on the project.

I strive for win/win situations. In this case, the owners get a new landscape and create good will and buzz that generates new business within the community; WRE gets a highly visible project to install within its market area thereby leading to new business.

Many of our residential and commercial landscape clients have become what I call "active advocate clients," that is, people who help fuel our company with new clients via testimonials. Literally 75 percent of our business comes from the personal referrals of 20 percent of our clients.

Persistence

One of the best illustrations of persistence is Winston Churchill's ascension to prime minister in 1940 after spending years criticizing the English government, pleading with parliament to increase its military forces and to be proactive to stop the spread of Nazism—all to deaf ears. But, with the persistence of a bulldog, Churchill was eventually elected to the position of prime minister and led England to victory over Hitler during WWII.

Achieving the goal of creating a comprehensive, award-winning, coastal landscape design, construction and maintenance firm was not easy. There were many obstacles to overcome, and there will be many more to deal with in the future. Through it all, however, my business goals served as a guiding light even during extremely difficult times.

Not one to give up, I persevered and succeeded.

LESSONS LEARNED:

1. Nothing extraordinary in life comes easy. Having a dream is one thing, living it is another. Clarify your vision and focus your eye on the prize while moving toward it.
2. Confidence comes with success AND failure. Create a culture where failure is secondary to learning and mistakes are forgiven. Surviving the maelstrom gives one the courage to brave another storm.
3. Be persistent. Milestones are made one step at a time.

CHAPTER 5
CREATE A SOUND BUSINESS PLAN

"By failing to prepare, you are preparing to fail."

Benjamin Franklin

In 1989, WRE had just finished its fourth fiscal year with billings of over $900,000 in gross sales. My goal of breaking a million dollars seemed closer than ever to becoming a reality. I believed that if I crossed that magical financial milestone, I would have finally made it—four years after leaving a secure job as a biology teacher and track coach. I had created a successful landscape construction business from ground zero. Who knew how high we could grow: $1.5 million? $2 million? Boy, was I wrong!

In 1990, our gross sales dropped 50 percent to $450,000, followed by an equally dismal $460,000 in 1991. I was stunned and unprepared. I laid off workers, sold equipment, and sought loans from my banks and several relatives. A very generous aunt kept me afloat with nothing but faith as collateral. My local bank, however, was not so forthcoming with financial help and bluntly suggested that I consider filing for bankruptcy.

There was no way I would declare bankruptcy (or admit failure), so I began to ask myself some tough questions: What went wrong? Why didn't I see it coming? Why wasn't I better prepared? How am I going to get this company back on track again?

My answer came in the form of a newsletter from my local bank, The Washington Trust Company. Buried in the other bank news was an advertisement for an eight-week seminar on how to write a business plan. I signed up. I was determined to create a plan that would set a course for my business, where it was going, and how I intended to get it there.

The class was enormously helpful and guided me through the process of setting goals and listing strategies to reach them. I developed a marketing plan, made financial projections, did a cash-flow analysis, and outlined my equipment, vehicle and labor needs. And then I created a contingency plan in case my primary plan didn't materialize.

I worked day and night until I had compiled a comprehensive business plan over the eight-week seminar. At the conclusion of the course, I presented the completed plan to my banker. After reviewing it, along with my financial request, he agreed to restructure my debt, establish a credit line for my business, and give our company the financial backing it needed to stay afloat and poised for the future.

What changed the bank's point of view? The business plan did. It clearly showed the direction in which we were headed, how we would meet our financial obligations, and it included a detailed contingency plan in case we didn't make our projections. It demonstrated that we were organized and gave the banker a sense of security, knowing we had a plan for growth and a means to achieve it. Within 60 days of submitting our plan and financial request, our debt was reorganized and a credit line was in place. Since that time, we have had an evolving business plan in place.

Over the years the business plan has performed numerous functions.

Critical Financial Data

Raising money is often a primary reason for writing a business plan and as I experienced, a well-thought out plan is an absolute requirement for getting funded by any professional banker or money manager.

There are many valuable books on the market that can guide you through the planning process. A favorite of mine is a simple workbook written by William Lasher, Ph.D., C.P.A., called *"The Perfect Business Plan Made Simple."* Lasher's easy-to-follow steps define financing basics and help you understand the differences between, and value of, financial statements, income statements, balance sheets, assets, liabilities, equity, the cash flow statement, cost ratio analysis, and cost accounting. The better one understands the role of these financial tools and how they relate to the business, the easier it is to make logical (and realistic) financial forecasts for the business. The financial component of the business plan is what bankers (and investors) focus on the most. You must be able to demonstrate your total understanding of the numbers.

A Benchmark To Track Success And Failure

Another function of the business plan is to alert the company when certain areas of the business aren't working.

When setting goals in the plan (sales increases or overhead reduction, new market penetration, new service offerings, etc.), be sure to gauge your current situation and use it as a benchmark to track your progress (or lack of it).

It is important to establish time and budget parameters at the outset of goal-setting, and be willing to pull the plug on any investment of energy, money, or labor that does not generate the desired return before reaching the end of those parameters.

Several times in the past five years certain business divisions were eliminated when they were no longer meeting our goals, particularly in the financial arena. The Mail-A-Wreath program, a mainstay for years in our Christmas business, was eliminated along with the Christmas tree business in 2003 because of lagging sales and financial losses. Our foray into the sprinkler business was brief due to a shortfall when it came to meeting our high standards of customer service and satisfaction as well as our financial goals.

Setting The Course For Future Growth

Our business plan also acts as a road map for our future: where are we now and where are we headed, how will we get there and what will we need along the way to achieve our goals, when will the process begin and how will we know we have reached our destination?

In the past, prior to the plan, employees were unclear as to the direction we were headed. Now, as the plan is communicated to the team and revised as needed with their input, the overall direction is clear and we are all working together to achieve the same goals.

Building On the Plan For Continued Success

Over time, we have updated the plan and expanded its contents. Eventually, it included an executive summary, vision and mission statements, current market analysis, an outline of products and services, an inventory of personnel along with job descriptions, and detailed financial data such as balance sheets, and profit and loss (P&L) and cash-flow statements.

With the plan as a benchmark we could track our growth and keep our eyes on the bottom line. As the business, markets and needs of our customers changed, we eliminated unprofitable divisions and expanded our more profitable landscape services. It is ironic that I hadn't considered a detailed plan for my own business prior to the early 1990s, yet I always insisted that our clients complete a landscape design and plan before we implemented a project on their behalf!

CHAPTER 6
PROFIT IS NOT A DIRTY WORD

"I don't want to do business with those who don't have a profit, because they can't give the best service."

Lee Bristol

A line from Bob Seger's song *"Runnin' Against the Wind"* defined for years how I felt trying to make a profit. Although I know that the financial matters of my business are vital to its continued success, I freely admit they are my least favorite activities. I would much rather visit with clients, assist in marketing efforts, speak at a garden club, or visit a local nursery supplier than meet, discuss and plan a budget, review financial updates, or plug in job-costing data.

To make financial tasks more palatable, I have put into place people and processes that allow me to balance the more "enjoyable" aspects of my job with the tedious job of managing money.

First, I hired and promoted extremely talented and dedicated employees who perform the key financial tasks of accounting, bookkeeping and estimating. I also hired top-notch accountants, financial advisors and consultants who collectively have created systems for job-costing actuals against the estimates, and who generate financial statements, corporate tax returns and detailed budget programs.

Second, the employees in key financial positions share computer systems, databases and software such as QuickBooks®, and all of our records are updated daily. This creates efficiencies in time and accuracy is ensured.

Our accounting manager, Jane Perry, meets with me each Wednesday over lunch away from the office to review current payables, receivables, upcoming projects, projected cash flow and any important employee/compensation issues that may arise. Since implementing these weekly meetings, my apprehension about financials has abated and we both look forward to discussing current financial needs and planning future steps.

Over the years, our budget program has become more sophisticated and now includes detailed reports on each truck, tractor, Kubota, etc., profiling loan-payment costs, taxes, fuel use, insurance fees, maintenance expenses, and a replacement value amount so that theoretically at the end of their useful existence, the vehicles not only will have paid for themselves, they will have generated enough money to purchase replacements.

Our director of operations, Mark Grenier, who is responsible for project estimates, created a new estimating program in Excel one winter. The program consists of several templates containing formulas that hold all current costs for materials, labor and vehicles. His formulas also incorporate our standard overhead percentage and desired profit margin.

Once Mark enters the amount of materials required to complete a job, and estimates labor hours and equipment, machine and vehicle hours, the template calculates a project estimate in seconds.

Along with a summary estimate sheet we use for billing purposes, the program also creates a summary sheet used by the team leaders and managers as a guideline for materials, machine and equipment time, and labor hours estimated to complete the job. As the project proceeds, team leaders and managers can track progress against the estimate, giving them a greater sense of direction and a method to keep projects on track budgetwise. Mark meets with me each morning to review the daily assignments and any job estimates he has prepared. The program he created has saved us considerable time and money.

Unfortunately, the most important component of our comprehensive system—job costing—has not been used to its full capacity. Our goal this year is to implement job costing 100 percent of the time for each project, large and small.

From my first financial setback, I have learned that being pro-active in my financial affairs is far better than reacting desperately to unexpected downfalls, cash-flow shortages and financial setbacks.

LESSONS LEARNED:

1. Hiring top-notch accounting managers, estimators, accounting firms, consultants, and financial advisers makes managing money less tedious.
2. Computerized processes for accounting, payroll, estimating, job costing and budgeting save time and money.
3. Financial reports help you keep an eye on the overhead and ensure the profit margin necessary to stay in business long-term.
4. Be pro-active in all financial decisions. Don't be afraid to ask for help from professionals.

CHAPTER 7
EXCEED CUSTOMER EXPECTATIONS

"When serving clients our goal is to not only meet their needs, but to exceed their expectations—every time!"

Frank Crandall

As many can testify, today's customer service rarely exceeds expectations. It may sometime meet our expectations, but most often service is downright dreadful: the coffee shop drive-through attendant who messes up your order, then makes you wait until someone can straighten out the problem; the cable service scheduled to arrive between 9 a.m. and noon but shows up at 2 p.m. without a call; the local bureaucrat at the registry who insists you haven't got the correct forms, dismisses you and calls for the next person in line. We all have experienced this level of customer service, and, as a result, have lowered our expectations. Today, "poor" service is the accepted norm.

From day one my company has had a different approach to customer service. Our motto is "to complete what we say we will within the time frame agreed on, and exceed client expectations—every time."

Our clients come to us to fulfill their needs: design a new landscape, build a stone wall, install a water feature or landscape lighting, plant an evergreen privacy screen, or maintain their landscape—and we strive to satisfy them. But, they also need to feel important, valued and respected for their ideas and input. Over the years I have identified things my clients value beyond the physical aspects of a specific job:

Make Customer Satisfaction Your #1 Priority

Why do we work so hard to keep customers satisfied? My experience shows that 20 percent of our established clients generate 75 percent of our gross sales. I think that's pretty good justification for keeping existing clients happy.

Before billing and after a project has been completed, the designer, construction team leader and I walk the landscape with the client to ensure that we have completed all that was proposed.

I make it a point to meet with all my clients at least once during the season to see how they are doing, make note of any special events coming up, discuss any problems, or review new projects.

We also keep in touch with our clients with a quarterly newsletter that introduces new products, services and personnel, and announces coming events at our facility. Our annual open house has become a featured event at the WRE Landscape Design Showcase, and clients enjoy the informative horticultural lectures, our themed gardens, and the exposure to new landscape elements such as pavers, lighting, golf greens and plants.

How else do we measure client satisfaction? We recently introduced a client survey card, which asks them to rate our services, products and attitudes on a scale of 1 to 4. With the results we can calculate an average score for each year, and set higher goals to exceed next year. Also, if there are problems, we can identify them soon after the project is done and make sure they are corrected.

Most of our design/build landscape projects result in property maintenance contracts after installation. We assign knowledgeable team leaders to visit the property each week and observe the overall health of the landscape, mow lawns, fertilize plantings, prune and communicate with the client on a regular basis to determine their needs.

In early February, we mail out detailed maintenance service check-off sheets to all our customers. The information generated by these forms helps us plan work schedules and budgets prior to the start of each new season.

Be Courteous: Return Phone Calls Promptly

Returning a client's phone call is not just courteous, it can set you apart from the competition. Many business people are slow to return calls; some never return them. Our company recently finalized a landscaping maintenance and construction agreement with a new client who came to us out of frustration after trying unsuccessfully to communicate with his previous landscaper. The client had called the landscaper several times over a period of three months to discuss some concerns he had. The landscaper never called the client back—until he was informed that his services would no longer be needed. Then he immediately called the client, oblivious to what the problems were, and proceeded to blame the client for the breakdown. Needless to say we are extremely fortunate to have this new client and will continue to communicate with him as often as needed—by phone and/or email, whichever method works best.

Take An Interest In Each Client

It is important to take a personal interest in your clients. Learn their names, the names of close family members and even the names of their pets! Find out their favorite sports, recent trips, etc., and begin to develop a relationship.

A major part of WRE's success can be attributed to the relationships we have built with clients over the years. Clients have become advocates of our success, finding additional projects for us to do even after their major projects have been completed. One landscape construction client bought a local restaurant and proceeded to renovate and expand it. We were called in to design, construct and maintain the newly refurbished landscape. No other firm was even considered.

Another client generously sent me to England to tour English gardens in May 2004 so I could learn more about her favorite gardening techniques and come away with ideas that I later applied in the landscape of her new home. I visited over 20 gardens, the 2004 Chelsea Flower Show, and many of London's historical sites. It was the trip of a lifetime for which I will be eternally grateful (and it rained for only one hour the whole trip). While on my tour I took over 1,100 digital pictures that have become the basis for numerous presentations.

Adopt A "No Problem" Attitude

When clients ask for the unusual, the difficult, or a customized project, embrace it! Anyone can do simple, standard foundation plantings, lawn installations and front walks. Complex projects help you grow and learn. The challenging projects excite our crews. They will research, plan and execute new projects with tremendous zeal and they thrive on the satisfaction and pride they feel when those projects are complete. We have wonderful clients who often give us challenging landscape projects. One asked us to locate and plant a 35-foot Kousa dogwood next to her parking area in a confined space and to transform a ravine that was used as a dump for brush into a series of ponds, streams and waterfalls. Each project was staggering at first, but was ultimately implemented successfully, to the delight of the client and the satisfaction of our team.

Meet Clients' Needs And Respect Their Deadlines.

This is the client service we strive to maintain above all else—meeting mutually agreed upon deadlines. With few exceptions, we have been successful in doing so. Our team works to meet every single deadline mutually set by WRE and a client. Some deadlines have been extremely nerve wracking, but our team always rises to the occasion to achieve what some think impossible.

A recent example was a landscape project that included a custom swimming pool with waterfalls, customized outdoor grill and fire pit, a new lawn and landscape plantings, landscape lighting, and an irrigation system. The client set a hard deadline of July 14—the day he had scheduled a surprise birthday party for his wife and over 100 guests. The pool contractor was running into delays and I needed at least two weeks before the July 14 deadline to install all the landscape plantings around it.

In the end, the pool was finished just four days before the party. Rising to the challenge, all our division managers got together and carefully coordinated an intensive schedule of work for the design, construction, masonry, lighting and maintenance teams. As a result, the project was completed in the four days we had left. The maintenance crew came in on the day before the event, cleaned up everything, planted annuals and waved goodbye as the caterers unloaded tables and tents! Without a talented, disciplined and passionate team brave enough to meet a daunting task head-on, this project never would have succeeded. The owner was so thrilled he gave our company a substantial bonus to be distributed to the team—and they were extremely appreciative.

Stand By Your Work

No matter what the project size, clients expect problems to be corrected without hesitation. WRE has a reputation for correcting problems, replacing plants or making requested changes to ensure that a client is happy. At times this has come at significant cost to our company, but it is essential if we are to remain in integrity with our clients. As one aspect of this policy, we offer a 5-year plant warranty. It is the leading guarantee in the industry. We have always been at the leading edge of customer service, offering the best service, the best warranty and the best quality product available. We don't succeed every time, but our goal remains exceeding expectations every time.

Remember To Say "Thank You!"

When our Christmas tree business was still open, we sent each landscape client a wreath in early December to show our appreciation for his or her support during the year. The response was always amazing. Many sent thank you cards, but more would call, giving us a chance to thank them in person.

Obviously client service is the backbone of our company. Who better to sum that up than the clients themselves? When testimonials come in, I personally read them to the entire team and post them in the office.

In his book *"The Secret,"* Ken Blanchard summarizes the value of good customer service: "If we can take care of our customers and create a motivating working environment for our people, profits and financial strength are the applause we get for a job well done!"

LESSONS LEARNED:

1. Make customer satisfaction your #1 priority.
2. Timely communication with clients is an essential ingredient to customer satisfaction.
3. Generate long-term client relationships by creating a personal connection and paying attention to details.
4. Adopt a "no problem" attitude when dealing with client requests.
5. Set deadlines and meet them.
6. Measure client satisfaction and set a goal to improve each year.
7. Always remember to say "Thank You!"

CHAPTER 8
BUILD A STRONG BRAND

"How your customers feel about your brand isn't a casual question. It is the critical question."

Daryl Travis - "Emotional Branding"

What Is A Brand?

A brand is a collection of many things: an expectation of performance, a mark of trust and integrity, a reputation, and a collection of memories. Today's buying decisions are made on promises that transcend products or services. The promises are rooted in human emotions. It's not about what you do; it's about what customers want, what motivates them to buy, and why they want to buy from you. A brand is not part of your business. It IS your business.

What Is The WRE Brand?

Although I have always been aware of the fundamental ingredients of a brand, I never fully comprehended the full value of our own brand until Lynda Martel joined our firm in 1998. She initially came on board as our nursery manager. Soon, however, she was handling all our marketing and became our brand champion. Her years of advertising and marketing experience, and previous position as director of worldwide corporate communication for GTECH, taught her that a well-recognized brand was important to all businesses.

Lynda undertook the tasks of strengthening our existing brand, increasing brand awareness in our markets, and creating relationships with customers that resulted in a preference for our brand. Her recommendations included the following:

• Refresh the WRE logo to reflect where the company had been and where it was going. Use it consistently across all communication vehicles (uniforms, letterhead, invoices, thank you cards, newsletters, advertising, signage, etc.)

• Define the brand's core value as the company's mission statement, promote its meaning to all employees, and emphasize their role in supporting the brand in terms of product quality, customer service and the promise of satisfaction.

• Develop a marketing plan to promote the brand message in existing and potential markets through the use of tactics such as radio ads, newsletters, company brochures, television exposure, garden club presentations, and speaking engagements at industry trade shows.

• Design an employee recruitment program that attracts hardworking, responsible, talented employees who embody the brand.

• Measure all our activities against the core values of the brand, promoting the idea that the brand is a living, dynamic entity that needs leadership, direction and defending.

Our brand loyalty is strong enough to provoke a call to us from clients when they're approached by our competition. Over 90 percent of our clients have been with us 10 years or more. Our logo has become well recognized and respected throughout southern New England.

Our brand is more than a symbol. It's a guarantee that a project will be of top quality, the team will be professional, courteous and fun to work with, we will warranty the work we do, and, should there be a problem, it will be corrected.

Our brand also holds value to our vendors and subcontractors, who recognize it for extremely quick service and quality work. Most of our subcontractors and vendors refer us for projects when their clients ask for recommended landscape companies. Obviously this is an ideal situation we all wish to foster: win, win.

Why Branding Is Important To Your Business

A strong brand can be leveraged when offering additional products or services for continued growth.

A strong brand sets a company apart from the competition. In our market, only our brand stands for an award-winning, full-service, coastal landscape design, construction and maintenance firm dedicated to exceptional customer service. We offer the industry's best warranty (five years) to prove it.

Striving to be the best landscape company in southern New England has set us apart from our competition and provides a secure footing in a market where our brand is top-of-mind.

Your brand is the most valuable asset your company owns. Internalize it from the way you answer the phone to the way your answer your conscience.

LESSONS LEARNED:

1. *Your brand is your business. Embrace it. Nurture it.*
2. *Create a brand identity for your company that will set it apart from the competition.*
3. *A strong brand generates customer loyalty.*
4. *Brand loyalty will help you survive market shifts and economic downturns.*
5. *Your brand is your most valuable asset.*

CHAPTER 9
DOMINATE YOUR MARKET

"Marketing is about creating relationships with your clients that result in a preference for your brand."

Lynda Martel

When I made the decision to start a Christmas farm and landscape business at my remote location in Woodville, R.I., I knew that marketing would be critical to attracting customers to our site.

We are in the country, but not that far from nearby areas more heavily populated. Woodville is a small village outside of Hope Valley, 10 miles north of Westerly, five miles south of Hope Valley, four miles from Interstate Route 95, 15 miles north of Stonington and Mystic, Conn. and 30 miles south of Providence, R.I.

In our little state, however, there is a perception that a destination longer than 30 minutes away is "just too far a drive." One of my biggest marketing challenges, therefore, was convincing nearby populations that traveling five, 10, or 25 miles into the country would be a safe, enjoyable, worthwhile trip. It never ceases to amaze me how many first-time visitors remark about the "journey" from Westerly to Woodville (a 10-minute drive) yet they willingly travel 25 to 30 miles to the malls. Once customers make the trip to our 12 pristine acres of country land surrounded by the beautiful Wood River and waterfalls, however, they agree it is worth the trip.

The retail aspects of our business, nursery, Christmas shop and tree farm, Spooky Halloween Hayride and Festival of Lights Hayride, required a significant marketing investment and a variety of techniques to attract the numbers of customers (and revenue) necessary to offset expenses and support the business.

I have always been fascinated with marketing techniques used by other businesses, and over the first 10 years I think I used most of them. Some of the more successful techniques we've used are newspaper advertising and radio ad campaigns, our own newsletter, our public relations efforts (interviews and press releases that generated feature articles), our annual open house event, Santa Claus (a great PR opportunity every season), and public speaking engagements at local garden clubs and trade shows.

Less successful for us were TV and cable ads, large promotional balloons, discount coupons, direct-mail promotions, the Web site and full-color product catalogs.

By far the most successful marketing technique in terms of client referrals and new business development has been a landscape we installed and continue to maintain at a highly visible gas station in Pawcatuck, Conn.

The Evans Mobil Phenomenon

In 1996 I drove into Evans Mobil Gas Station in Pawcatuck, Conn. to get gas. The owner, Ellison Evans, approached me and asked if I could design, install, and maintain a landscape in a small plot of land bordering his parking lot at the junction of Liberty Street (Route 2) and Route 1.

This spot, although small, generated huge traffic counts on a daily basis. Ellison wanted a landscape that would attract attention, look professional, improve the appearance of his business property, have color and interest all year long, and "be the talk of the town." I thought about it for five seconds and gladly accepted the challenge.

My landscape designer Mary Jo Girard and I designed and installed a special landscape that met all of Ellison's demands. The 65- by 12-foot corner island space featured graceful contours, vibrant perennials, an evergreen tree, small waterfalls, and several grassy areas.

This striking garden display at Evans Mobil is located at a busy intersection in Pawcatuck, Conn.

The most unique features of the landscape were the areas designated for seasonal changeovers. The changeover areas were teeming with crocus, tulips and daffodils that brightened the landscape in spring. Pots of pansies, which last until the summer changeover in June, were planted amongst the bulbs for a continuous display of color.

For summer, we replaced the pansies with New Guinea impatiens, scaevola and petunias—in colors that matched Mobil's corporate colors of red, white and blue.

In September, the fall changeover design featured the gold and yellow hues of mums and asters interspersed with kale used for their interesting texture and long life span.

The winter/Christmas changeover is the highlight of our seasonal changeover program. Each year we transform Ellison's island landscape into a special Christmas scene. In addition to replacing the mums with pots of evergreen boughs, the planting beds and gas station are decorated with red bows and lights, roping and wreaths. We place 8-foot Fraser Fir trees throughout the island and decorate them with red bows and lights. And a sleigh loaded with gifts and pulled by a reindeer is placed in full view of the main road.

From year to year, our selection of annuals is changed to maintain interest. Seasonal decorations such as pumpkins, reindeer, birdhouses and such are used to accent each floral display. Some decorations are handcrafted and one-of-a-kind.

Over the years, Evans Mobil has won numerous awards from the Greater Westerly-Pawcatuck Chamber of Commerce. Our company has won several awards from the Rhode Island Nursery and Landscape Association and the Rhode Island Monthly magazine in recognition of this landscape design and installation.

No one could have predicted the incredible success of this small island planting. Ellison is constantly calling me to pass along compliments he receives from pedestrians who pass by and customers who drive into his station. Students from the local middle school wrote letters to Ellison commending him for improving the downtown area. The landscape has generated many published newspaper articles, photographs and feature stories. And the local community was motivated to improve other downtown areas with landscaping, including the planting of state-owned roadside islands.

The Evans Mobil landscape has done several things for our company: it raised the visibility of our work within one of our key market areas; it led to numerous other commercial changeover projects; it generated awards of recognition for our business; it became a great creative outlet and source of pride to our staff; it provided something special to the community; and it has produced over 90 client referrals for our business, representing significant project-related revenues.

The Evans Mobil phenomenon proves that marketing doesn't have to involve an expensive advertising program or four-color brochure; it can be one high-profile project done in a location frequented by a large number of your customers.

In return for the marketing value our company receives from Evans Mobil, we extend to Ellison a significant discount on the four changeovers, which helps him maintain his desired goals and provides WRE with the opportunity to showcase our work year-round. Potential clients are much more likely to call you if they see examples of your work and that work is consistently outstanding and creative.

Frank The Shameless Marketer

The need to promote our company to new and existing clients has been a major focus of mine—perhaps to the extreme. I always carry my business cards and company brochures. You never know when a marketing opportunity will present itself.

In October of 1998, while running our Spooky Halloween Hayride, we experienced a rain-out. Taking advantage of this night off, a group of us went to the Steak Loft Restaurant in Mystic, Conn. for a well-deserved meal. We had been working 16 to 18 hours a day during the hayride/landscape season. After the meal, I went into the rest room, and before leaving stuck one of our magnetic Spooky Halloween Hayride cards on a bathroom stall wall. I never thought any more about it.

Four days later a customer for the hayride was asked at the ticket counter how he heard about us. He chuckled and said "You won't believe this, but I found your number on a magnetic card in the men's room at the Steak Loft." Needless to say, I never heard the end of it from my staff for my "shameless marketing."

The Power Of Free Press

An effective, low-cost (and perhaps more refined) method of marketing that has worked well for us is public relations.

Lynda Martel has used a variety of techniques to gain free publicity for our company. Numerous newspaper articles have been printed about our business, its growth and our special seasonal events.

This type of coverage is accomplished by developing relationships with local newspaper editors. We provide them with well-written information from which to develop a story, and we often submit press kits containing photos and background information about our company and its special events.

We also invite editors to visit our WRE Landscape Design Showcase, which is always a source of good photo opportunities for seasonal horticultural and gardening information. We keep in touch regularly, and sincerely thank them for any coverage we receive. Over the years, the free publicity WRE has received has been worth its weight in gold.

Another effective PR technique is to become the "expert" in a specific area or on a specific topic. During one season of drought, I submitted tips on water conservation and proper watering techniques to local papers in communities that were experiencing watering bans.

Many times we have parlayed our expertise into guest appearances on radio or TV talk shows, or into invitations to speak at local garden clubs, universities and trade shows. Through a relationship with the University of Rhode Island's Cooperative Extension-Plant Sciences Department we are often invited to appear as a guest on the televised program "Plant Pro," a regular feature on NBC's local TV Channel 10.

This type of publicity technique comes natural to me. For years I have enjoyed speaking at green industry events. It allows me to pursue my love of teaching and share my passion about plants, landscaping and preserving the environment. Though not the primary goal, speaking and teaching frequently generate new clients who contact WRE after attending a lecture or after learning about landscape design.

Giving Back To Your Community

Civic marketing—helping others in the community—has been another main element of our public relations program. I feel a strong obligation to give back to my local community. I have donated products and services to the The Greater Westerly-Pawcatuck Chamber of Commerce to be used in their landscape; installed a memorial garden for the fallen firemen of the Ashaway Fire Department; donated time and materials to the McCourt Memorial Garden commemorating 9/11 victims from the New London area; donated materials and equipment to the Angel Memorial Project at Westerly Hospital; and in memory of a deceased member of our team, we run an annual golf tournament that supports the Lianne Maher Memorial Scholarship Fund which provides financial assistance in the form of scholarships to area high school seniors bound for college in pursuit of a career in education or horticulture. I am happy to participate in these worthy causes and will continue to give so that others can have opportunities like those I have had.

At the root of our marketing success is our marketing plan. The plan outlines our short- and long-term goals, marketing objectives and strategies, and sets a course of action to follow with built-in benchmarks that help us measure progress as we strive to reach our goals.

Seasons change, people change and market conditions change, requiring adjustments in your plan to reflect those changes. Each winter we re-evaluate our goals for the next season and set new strategies if needed. By continually revisiting our marketing plan, we can adjust or refine our tactics so that only the most effective marketing techniques are used to achieve our goals.

LESSONS LEARNED:

1. Marketing plays a critical role in the establishment, growth, and success of your business.
2. Through research (trial and error), you can discover which advertising techniques work best for your company.
3. Installing a high-profile project in a location populated by and visible to your customers is a great tool to generate new business referrals and goodwill in the communities you serve.
4. Public relations can be your best source of advertising—and it's free!
5. Civic marketing is a way of giving back to your community and sharing the blessings you've had in life.

CHAPTER 10
MOTIVATE CLIENT REFERRALS

"Good will plus good service brings sales success that no competition can possibly undersell."

Harry F. Banks

One obvious goal of our marketing plan is to attract new clients. The most effective way to generate new clients is from existing happy clients who gladly recommend our company to friends and business contacts. Client referrals have fueled our company's growth for the past 20 years.

How does one motivate client referrals? You start with outstanding customer service. Very satisfied clients will not only mention your name to friends, they will provide an active, enthusiastic endorsement of you, your company, and its products and services.

I call individuals who endorse our company "active client advocates" because they are not only very satisfied with our work but they have developed a rapport with members of our team, trust we will do what we say, and have a sincere desire to see us grow and succeed. Our satisfied customers, along with our most loyal subcontractors, vendors and staff, have become a valuable marketing team.

While installing a large landscape for a new customer this past summer, for example, the customer asked if we could move some boulders from his neighbor's yard to the edge of our client's steep drive for safety reasons. We readily agreed and the next day began to move the boulders with our Kubota loader. The client spoke with the neighbor during the day to confirm that everything was OK, and the neighbor was thrilled to be rid of the pile of boulders.

During their conversation, the neighbor commented on the quality of the landscaping and asked who was completing the work? Our client answered, "Wood River Evergreens," to which the neighbor responded, "They do great work, but aren't they expensive?"

I wish I could have recorded my customer's exact reply. It went something like this:

"We hired WRE to complete a master plan, which they did according to our needs. They told us they would begin the project on Tuesday at 9 a.m., and the crews showed up at 8:30 a.m. that day. The team was extremely professional, stayed until the job was completed, and finished before the estimated deadline. The owner called us regularly to see if everything was OK, gave me an overall discount on the project because I agreed to complete it all at once, and extended to me a 5-year warranty on all the plantings. With the value of service they provided, they were worth every penny."

For the past four years, we have subcontracted Ted Richards, owner of Pools by Richard, for all our swimming pool projects. Ted completes spectacular, custom-designed pools incorporating the latest in pool technology. WRE often assists his company with landscape designs that border the pools, coordinates site excavation and trenching, constructs pool decking and installs the landscape plantings.

Ours has been a mutually beneficial relationship for both companies. We have referred Ted to several other clients with pool projects, and, in turn, Ted has recommended our services to his clients because "they are extremely professional, do superb work, and for the value they bring to the project, are the best I've ever worked with."

Don't Let That Hot Prospect Get Cold

Once you have been given a referral, it is important to contact them within 24 hours—preferably the same day they called. When you contact the prospect, remember to focus on them and what they need. Be interesting as well as interested. Listen carefully, offer helpful solutions and be prompt with your follow-up. Set up a convenient meeting time to discuss their project. In the meantime, provide them with your branded marketing materials and any other information they request about your company.

At the first meeting it is important to establish a rapport and begin to develop a relationship. The saying that you only have one opportunity to make a first impression is true. When meeting with new customers, I try to apply what Jeffrey H. Gitomer, author of *"The Sales Bible,"* refers to as the "wow factor." I strive to be positive, prepared, genuine, enthusiastic, focused, funny, knowledgeable, compelling, and most of all—memorable!

After the initial meeting, with all needs identified, define a plan to meet those needs. Schedule a personal follow-up meeting to go over your plan and to review your detailed estimate. Be professional. Have the estimate and proposal neatly prepared. Be on time (preferably five minutes early). And, if you cannot be on time, make a call.

Close The Sale With Ease

Before reviewing estimated project cost figures I usually make a humorous remark like: "I'm so pleased the estimate was only three times as high as your budget!" Usually, this gets a hearty laugh, releases tension and we can move on in comfort. (Once, however, this approach created a nervous reaction with one client's wife who later confessed that she was ready to show me the door before I even went over the figures.)

When going through the estimate, it is essential to demonstrate solutions to their problems, provide compelling reasons for the solutions, and be ready with answers to any objections that might arise. Objections actually indicate interest and by skillfully handling them you will eventually be in a position to ask for the sale.

Sometimes, in phased projects, the clients debate amongst themselves whether to complete phase one, two, or the whole installation. At the appropriate time, I offer a discount for completing all project phases, and excuse myself while I go to my truck to get a contract. This gives the clients a chance to discuss in private what they want to do. Most times they accept the discounted proposal and we sign the contract right then. (Always have a contract with you. Without a signed contract, a project is only tentative.)

Although a signed contract is a significant milestone in the sales process, it is not the end. Stay in constant touch with the client to notify him or her of start dates, to verify material selections, or to ask additional questions to help ensure a smooth job.

Deliver On The Promise

Most important: deliver what you promise! Nothing destroys client goodwill faster than not showing up when scheduled, not installing what was specified, or not providing the quality of product or service expected. I look at every project, small or large, as a long-term proposition meaning that I want every detail to be carefully taken care of so that our new client becomes an "active client advocate."

Once a project is done, I walk around the property with the client to observe the results, see and hear the client's reactions, and identify any loose ends. Once final payment is made, we mail out a customer survey card to solicit feedback and, hopefully, generate new testimonials of a job well done. This is also the time to send a personal thank you card to the client who referred the new customer to your business. A gift certificate to a local restaurant might also be in order.

Referrals from satisfied customers can be a less expensive method of generating new business than the cost of advertising and promotional materials. A significant investment in excellence and 100 percent customer satisfaction, however, must be made.

Referrals we receive typically result in an 85 percent closing rate, certainly much higher than the industry average of 33 percent. This speaks volumes about practicing techniques and policies that help you retain existing clients and the importance of regularly communicating with them.

In the end, I want our clients to applaud our services and products, acclaim their experience with WRE, and advocate our company and team to their friends, neighbors and associates.

LESSONS LEARNED:

1. *Create "active client advocates" by keeping clients satisfied.*
2. *Do what you promise.*
3. *Return phone calls and e-mails the same day you receive them.*
4. *When meeting with new clients, listen carefully, be interested (as well as interesting), passionate about what you do, genuine, helpful, knowledgeable and memorable.*
5. *Be prompt in all your business dealings. If you are going to be late, call.*
6. *Always have a contract with you. Approval of an estimate is tentative until a contract is signed and a deposit received.*
7. *Send a thank you note to the customer after a project has been completed; it's a great way to show your appreciation for the work.*

CHAPTER 11
FOSTER A WINNING COMPANY CULTURE

"All your strength is in union, all your danger is in discord."

Henry Wadsworth Longfellow

Our company culture is rooted in the basic principles of integrity, honesty, fairness, compassion, dedication, creativity, tolerance, customer service, hard work, positive reinforcement, mutual respect, professionalism and loyalty. With these principles embedded in our management philosophy and mission statement, we attract, hire and retain employees sure to embody our brand value and become part of a winning team.

It is important for every individual to be in alignment with our principles and values for our culture to remain harmonious and happy.

Regardless of the business, the owner sets the tone for the company culture through the management philosophy and the company's mission statement.

WRE Management Philosophy:

Our management philosophy, as stated in our business plan, is as follows:

The success of Wood River Evergreens is rooted in our commitment to provide outstanding customer service and the finest products available to enhance the beauty, value, safety and health of their residential or commercial landscapes. Our customers will always come first, and we will treat each one with respect and courtesy.

To support our commitment to quality and customer satisfaction, we will hire talented, professional, dedicated employees with a penchant for quality and the desire to be part of an award-winning team. We will attract and retain such employees by fostering a company culture that advocates participatory management, rewards honesty and integrity, emulates a close family atmosphere, provides a safe and healthy work environment, offers opportunities for continuing education, job diversification, professional growth, competitive wages and benefits in exchange for energetic, thorough and dependable work.

The WRE Mission Statement:

> *Wood River Evergreens, Inc. is dedicated to providing award-winning landscape design, installation, lighting, and maintenance solutions to customers in Rhode Island and southeastern Connecticut who wish to enhance the beauty, value, safety, and health of their seaside and coastal landscapes.*
>
> *Our customers will always come first. We know that their satisfaction is directly connected to our long-term success. We will treat each client with respect and courtesy, perform each job with integrity, and deliver the utmost in quality—consistently.*

Our management philosophy and mission statement are the result of many influences, particularly my track and cross-country coaching experiences at Killingly High School and Chariho High School.

Coaching shaped many of the basic values and management principles that I practiced while developing my business. Motivating athletes, managing team members and assistant coaches, acknowledging each success, supporting and providing encouragement, team training and discipline are all skills that were easily transferred to the management and development of WRE.

Supporting The Company Culture In Many Roles

I find myself challenged daily to perform numerous roles to keep team members, clients and vendors, satisfied and happy. Although the role I am most comfortable with is that of coach, I find that each day I must play other roles as well (including psychologist) as I try to figure out the motives behind the unreasonable behavior of some employees. Often I also play the role of counselor. Except in serious cases, where I refer the employee to a licensed professional, I sit quietly and listen to an employee's story about his family situation, medical problems, or other daily trials and tribulations.

I relish my role as an educator (Once a teacher, always a teacher!) and organize a variety of outlets to satisfy this love. We hold workshops for staff members to advance their knowledge of horticultural information, proper planting or pruning techniques, business information such as cost estimating, and career advancement workshops such as landscape lighting or golf green sales and installation.

Whenever possible, I share horticultural and plant maintenance information with my clients. I have offered workshops at my facility to teach landscape design, proper landscaping techniques and the value to the environment of a well-designed, healthy landscape. Periodically I help teach a landscape management class at the local university, and speak to horticultural organizations like The Master Gardeners and community garden clubs.

Another role I have to play occasionally is that of banker. In times of financial crisis, a business owner is sometimes the only one an employee can turn to for support, and I get requests to lend them some money until payday, or to help with a family crisis. Lending money can lead to uncomfortable situations. I have learned to keep track of any money I do lend to an employee, and to outline payment terms at the outset. I also try to advise them on how to prevent future shortfalls by budgeting.

A particularly difficult role to perform (for me at least) is that of disciplinarian. Over the years, I have learned to enforce rules in a firm but fair way. I know that there are two sides to each situation, and extensive fact-finding is required before making judgment. It is amazing what a day or two of contemplation can do to influence a result.

If you're in business long enough, professional relationships often develop into friendships. If your company culture promotes a team and family environment, you will soon share in your employees' personal successes and milestones, setbacks and tragedies. (I've given four eulogies for employees who have passed on.)

Sometimes the value of long-term employees requires adjustments that allow them to serve the business in a different role. One of my employees has been with our company for 12 years. Arthritis required him to have a hip replaced at age 48 and he was concerned he wouldn't be able to keep up with the rigorous physical activities required in a landscape construction business.

At the time our business had grown to the point where I could no longer manage all the roles I had previously handled daily. I needed a talented, hard-working, trusted employee to do the estimates, and ultimately run the business while I was away. I offered him the position of director of operations—a new position that he filled admirably—and this long-term employee has been able to remain with us and help us to continue to grow.

I'm reminded of John C. Maxwell's quote, "Loyalty fosters unity, and unity breeds team success." The loyalty exhibited to and by our employees has a unifying effect on the whole team. There are lyrics from the Eagle's song "Hotel California" that say "... you can check out any time you want, but you can never leave." I joke with all my valuable employees and tell them they can't quit nor can they be fired, which is simply my way of letting them know how important they are to WRE and me.

Because most of us spend more hours at work than we do in our own homes, our company strives to attract a group of individuals who will be supportive and caring of one another. Here are some of the things we do that support that goal:

- Create a strong team spirit in a familylike environment.
- Communicate with all employees on a daily basis.
- Be attentive and aware of employee concerns. (How are the families doing? How's everyone's health? Any birthdays coming up? Anniversaries? Births?)
- Let them know you care.

Another key principle to a winning company culture is to set up each employee for success. Nothing is more demoralizing to a team than not having all the tools needed to complete a task. I firmly believe that when my team members head out to design or install a landscape, they will succeed even under the most difficult conditions because they have the resources to complete the project effectively and efficiently.

Over the years, with very few exceptions, I have provided team members with whatever they have requested to do their jobs: tools, equipment, vehicles, office supplies, skills and resources.

Diverse Uniformity

I will be the first to admit that not all employees in our company are treated the same—although there are core rules and principles that apply to each team member (and the owner).

Some job positions such as designers and office staff, however, allow for different work schedules, flextime, or the ability to work on projects at home. Flexibility on the part of a company helps employees who are single parents and who have obligations like picking up their children at day care or staying at home with them when they're sick or on vacation.

This difference in work schedules can cause clashes with employees who perform other functions, such as the managers, construction and maintenance workers, and masons whose jobs require them to report to work very early every single day. To help overcome this, I have held several team-building workshops to generate a greater level of respect for each function through education and understanding. Results have been encouraging. I continue to stress to all our employees that everyone is essential to the success of our team, regardless of job function or work schedule.

A diverse culture also requires a variety of motivational tools. I have found some employees motivated by bonuses, others by time off, personal recognition or new job titles. The important point is to recognize the diversity of your team within uniform guiding principles and to treat each employee in a way that leads him or her to success.

LESSONS LEARNED:

1. The owner sets the tone for a company's culture with management philosophy, mission statement and daily actions.
2. The owner's values must be in alignment with the company culture and the employees' values and principles in order to develop a cohesive team.
3. The owner must be able to effectively perform various roles: businessman, coach, psychologist, counselor, banker, educator and disciplinarian.
4. A healthy company culture can be created by boosting the morale of employees, cultivating team spirit and creating a family atmosphere.
5. Motivate, encourage, and set employees up for success.
6. Recognize the diversity of team members and treat them accordingly to achieve optimum success.

CHAPTER 12
ATTRACT, HIRE, RETAIN KEY EMPLOYEES

"Year-round growth, success and profitability as a company are directly related to the attitude, talent and motivation of your employees."

Frank Crandall

The number one complaint I hear from business owners I meet is how difficult it is to find good employees. And, if they are fortunate enough to find one, it is extremely difficult (if not impossible) to retain them.

A sustained, focused commitment is required to attract, hire and retain valuable employees. The success of WRE is directly related to the outstanding employees I've hired over the years. What steps do we use to build a winning team of employees? Why are our hiring techniques so effective?

When hiring, I look for talented, motivated and exceptional people who share our values, who can align themselves with our management philosophy, mission and vision for the company, and who will thrive personally and professionally within our company culture.

In a family-oriented culture, the hiring process is designed to ensure a match. The following steps have proven successful for developing our team:

Create A Culture That Supports A Winning Team

In recent years, WRE has attracted former landscape business owners, a worldwide marketing communications director, retired workers, and top-level employees from local and national companies like GTECH, Pfizer and Electric Boat (General Dynamics). Why? The main attraction is our relaxed work atmosphere, the positive, friendly, supportive environment, and our top-quality products and professional services. Advertising and networking may attract top-notch employees, but it is the company's culture that retains them.

Look Professional, Attract Professionals.

Our brand stands for quality, service and the promise of satisfaction. This reputation has permeated the southern New England market region. Potential employees (just like our preferred landscape clients) are attracted to our firm because we install only top-quality products, provide outstanding client service, and offer the industry's best warranty. Our well-dressed staff, new trucks and equipment, manicured company grounds, courteous and knowledgeable employees all contribute to our distinctive, professional image. Our brand image is reflected in every thing we do. Employees want to be a part of a winning team. We emphasize the benefits of working outdoors with plants, beautifying the environment, and being part of a growing horticultural industry that represents a significant economic part of the local agricultural community.

Be Specific About Job Requirements

Over the past five years, we have created formal job descriptions for all positions at WRE. Each job description outlines the job title, duties, requirements, responsibilities, job level, pay scale, benefits package and chain of command. With these concise descriptions, employees understand their role, feel empowered to fulfill their duties, and can see the requirements for leadership positions if they desire to move up within the company. To further enhance the perceived value of all team members, job titles were changed to remove the "bottom rung" connotations such as "laborer." Changing this title to "apprentice" or "craftsman" suggests a career path for the new employee versus a dead-end job. By having various job levels, an individual can increase his responsibilities, moving up the pay scale and increasing available unit days as a result. For instance:

WRE Job Levels:
Level One:
- Landscape Apprentice
- Clerk

Level Two:
- Landscape Craftsman
- Administrative Assistant

Level Three:
- Team Leader
- Executive Assistant

Level Four:
- Senior Team Leader

Level Five:

- Team Division Manager

Level Six:
- Directors
- Designers
- Owner

Job seekers responded favorably to our ads for "Landscape Apprentice" and "Landscape Craftsman" positions as opposed to "Landscape Laborer." The first set of applicants remarked that they were excited to have an opportunity to learn landscaping and were eager to meet their mentor/teacher. The result of the job description change has been incredible. We now attract a higher qualified, more motivated applicant.

The language in our employment ads specifies our hiring needs by listing available job positions. We advise applicants to bring a resume or an outline of their work history to the interview. The result has been a dramatic elevation of the quality of applicants responding to our ads, and increased success at attracting and hiring desirable employees.

Once individuals apply for a job, they fill out an extensive application form, which is then reviewed by the director of operations and team managers. Potential candidates are called in for the first screening interview with the director as well as the division managers the new candidate will work for. This interview lasts anywhere from 20 to 30 minutes and allows us to explore an applicant's professional background, experience and overall work ethic. It also allows us the opportunity to explain the job requirements and duties, WRE operations, its culture, values, management style and vision.

At the completion of the interviews, the management team rates the candidates and recommends those they wish to hire. These candidates are then scheduled to come in for a final interview with the director, appropriate division manager and owner. More detailed questions are asked to measure the applicant's ability to think on his/her feet, deal with potential conflicts on the job, and to outline benefits, set pay rates, and establish a start date. Before we offer candidates a job, all references are checked. Each new employee must complete a 90-day probation period before certain benefits (unit days and health plans) are available.

Sources For New Employees

• Ask current employees for referrals.

I have found that current employees are a great source of new recruits. They understand the company's needs, management style, the company culture and its diverse personality types, and usually demonstrate great insights on who might be a good match for our team.

Although I do not recruit competitors' employees, we do sometimes receive applications from employees of other landscape firms looking for opportunities to join our company. They are treated the same way as any other applicant and through the years we have hired several who have been excellent additions to our team.

Our local university (University of Rhode Island) has been a great source of potential employees including landscape designers, horticulturalists, turf specialists, team leaders and apprentices. Two of our landscape designers are graduates from URI's Landscape Architecture Department with which we maintain close ties as a resource for future hires. Our landscape architect, Jenn Judge, has taught a course on the fundamentals of landscape design at URI and is another great referral source for our firm. I serve as a guest lecturer for several of the horticulture classes at URI, and often class members have become WRE applicants.

Speaking at various public events, appearing on NBC TV's Channel 10 "Plant Pro" segment, assisting the Master Gardener's program and attending RINLA's educational seminar, have provided great networking opportunities to discuss WRE's employee needs, especially management positions.

• Host your own job fair.

In 1999, we realized that placing ads in local newspapers in early March to recruit new employees put us up against numerous other landscape firms also advertising for new recruits. Looking for more productive recruiting alternatives, we decided to host our own job fair in early February—well before help-wanted ads saturate the newspapers.

Our managers, team leaders and designers are on site at the WRE Job Fair to meet each new applicant. Staff members hand out sample landscape plans, show applicants photos and videos of our projects, talk to them about job roles and growth opportunities, and offer them refreshments. Results of this approach have been encouraging, and although we haven't attracted huge numbers of applicants we have hired key personnel before they were exposed to other newspaper ads in March. The job fair continues to elevate the importance we place on hiring new employees and has helped build up resume files.

The WRE Job Fair is promoted through local newspaper ads, flyers, local university horticultural classes, a statewide employment website and networking efforts with our employees who bring in potential applicants.

Create A Company Handbook

Whether you have three or 30 employees, you need a company handbook. This manual explains your mission, goals, philosophy, the nature of employment, employee job descriptions, benefit programs, payroll, working conditions, policies and procedures, rules of conduct, and other specifics including legal guidelines for handling conflicts, or leaves of absence.

WRE has had a handbook since 1994. It is a written guide we update each year and we hand one to every employee at the orientation session before every new season. We require that each employee read the handbook and sign the employee acknowledgement form within it. The form is kept on file in the office. The handbook has proven invaluable during company audits or when negotiating discipline measures and termination issues. The handbook also serves as a recruiting and educational tool for job candidates.

One essential ingredient of the handbook is the code of behavior, which all employees must follow.

- 100 percent customer satisfaction, 100 percent of the time
- Reflect our brand image
- Support WRE's mission each day
- Work with integrity
- Be accountable and responsible for your actions
- Use polite, professional language at all times
- Dress properly and appropriately for the task at hand
- Be on time all the time
- Respect your teammates
- Foster team spirit

Create Opportunities For Advancement

One of the advantages of the specific job descriptions is the detailed explanation of what is required for each position. An employee determined to advance within the company can review and pursue the courses, certification or other educational requirements necessary to apply for a new position.

WRE regularly sends employees to local horticultural conferences sponsored by the Rhode Island Nursery and Landscape Association (RINLA), New England Grows, URI's Cooperative Extension and others where they gain training and certification. Locally run workshops and adult education classes offer a variety of useful topics, such as computer use, perennial growing and management techniques. Our in-house training sessions have included database operation and development, accounting practices, inventory control, job estimating, pruning techniques, plant identification and landscape design.

WRE pays one-time bonuses for obtaining licenses and horticultural certification including R.I. certified horticulturalist, Connecticut and Rhode Island commercial pesticide certification, arborist certification, Commercial Driver License (CDL), lighting designer certification, Landscape Architect (LA) licensing, and Northeast Organic Farming Association (NOFA) Organic Land Care Accreditation.

Competitive Compensation

Instrumental to attracting and retaining employees is a competitive pay scale. Over the past five years, we have assigned pay rates to specific job descriptions and levels that are in the upper 10 percent of comparative landscape companies our size in New England. This pay scale and our competitive hiring practice has led to higher starting wages for new employees, and has resulted in wage adjustments for current employees who were hired many years earlier at a lower wage.

We have found, however, that certain other adjustments can be made to satisfy employees such as additional benefits (health and dental), more unit days for those who value time off, and new positions for those seeking advancement.

• Offer health benefits

I personally believe everyone who works at WRE should

have health insurance coverage. After a 90-day probation period, any employee not already covered by a health insurance plan can choose to enter our program. Due to substantial cost increases over the past three years, we have settled on a 50/50 split of the yearly cost. The employees pay their half through regular payroll deductions.

Approximately 85 percent of our team is laid off for the season from late December until mid-March. During this time off, WRE continues to pay 50 percent of the yearly fee, but the employee's 50 percent was collected during the previous work season through extra payroll deductions. This is an important benefit to seasonal workers, as they do not have to struggle paying for this important benefit when out of work. If an employee does not return the next work season, he or she is liable for the portion of winter health plan costs contributed by WRE. Over the years, we have experienced only one or two problems with this policy, and compensation was worked out mutually. I feel our health benefit plan is a significant reason for our low employee-turnover rate. Close to 90 percent of our employees return each year.

Continuing to pay for health plan coverage during the winter is a costly item for WRE, but it is far cheaper than hiring and training new employees each year. Clients appreciate that the same employees will be tending their landscapes year after year. Client satisfaction depends on skilled, experienced, motivated employees. We ensure this with our low turnover rate.

• Offer profit sharing

As our workforce aged (our employees range in age from 20 to 60), we realized that a retirement fund was in order. In 1996 we began a 401K account but later switched to a Simple IRA account which requires no owner limits or detailed reporting, allows for higher contribution limits, lets employees determine where to invest, and allows WRE to match up to 3 percent of the employee's contribution. This profit sharing plan has proved valuable to the employees (especially those of us aged 40-55). It is also much easier for me to implement, and is a great benefit to include in our compensation package.

• Offer Unit Days for Paid Time Off

As the business grew and new employees were added (most

full-time seasonal, some full time, some year-round), it became more difficult to equitably set standards for sick days, personal time, grievance time, vacation, etc., so I implemented the concept of unit days (eight hours of paid unit time), which could be used for any purpose and was assigned in amounts that correlated with each position, full-time, part-time or seasonal.

With few exceptions, this has simplified the whole time-off process. Also, when laid off in December, seasonal employees are paid for their unused unit time, giving them a financial bridge between their last week's paychecks and their first unemployment checks.

• Offer opportunities for continuing education

We also pay our staff to attend industry meetings, trade shows and educational seminars. Besides the instructive value of such events, employees get to learn about new products from exhibitors and get to network with fellow horticulturalists.

• Offer flextime scheduling

Several job functions allow completing certain projects at home or working on a variable time schedule. Such job functions are often attractive to employees who are raising families. Flextime schedules can be used to allow parents to care for children, or compensate them with more time off to make up for late-meeting attendance, or, in our case, on-site night-lighting customer visits.

Create Employee Events

In order to foster team spirit and a familylike environment, we schedule several employee events during the year: picnics, employee banquets, end-of-season Christmas party. Some of these events are scheduled just for fun, some to acknowledge employees for their achievements and to hand out bonus checks, and others to report the company's accomplishments and set goals for the upcoming year.

Help Employees Set Goals, Measure Performance

I feel strongly that a fair and comprehensive evaluation system can improve performance and identify areas that need to be addressed.

(Chapter 13 is dedicated to describing our evaluation program and process for goal setting with employees.)

Keep Your Team Motivated

The best two words you can use to motivate employees to complete a project, make a special effort, receive a client compliment, solve a problem, or make a suggestion that improves the company are "thank you." I want employees, the staff, and their families to know that their efforts are appreciated. I typically will thank an employee individually and in front of the staff, and sometimes will write a thank you note to let the family know as well. You will be amazed at the results generated from positive reinforcement.

Although I make substantial investments in new equipment, tools and vehicles, I always invest in my team in wages, benefits, training, mentoring, bonuses and profit sharing. Happy, secure, appreciated employees are a company's most valuable assets.

LESSONS LEARNED:

1. Attracting, hiring and retaining outstanding employees are possible with a focused commitment.
2. If your company's image looks professional you will attract high-quality candidates for hire.
3. Design job titles and related work responsibilities to attract candidates with qualifications the position needs.
4. Hosting your own job fair is a good way to attract many candidates and build up your resume files.
5. A company handbook is necessary, regardless of how many employees you have.
6. Retain employees by offering them opportunities for advancement, continuing education, and rewards for advanced certifications, licenses and accreditation.
7. Offer competitive pay and compensation packages as well as team-building employee events.

CHAPTER 13
MEASURE EMPLOYEE PERFORMANCE

"The key to developing people is to catch them doing something right."

Ken Blanchard and Spencer Johnson
- "The One Minute Manager"

One of the most difficult—and one of the most important—elements of our employee retention program is the yearly performance evaluation.

Clear, fair and comprehensive performance evaluations are necessary to let employees know where they stand in terms of job performance, promotions, wage increases, bonuses and specific areas of improvement. The aim of our evaluation system is to accurately "measure" job performance in 10 categories, reward accomplishments, identify areas for improvement, and set goals for advancement. The ultimate goal of our system is professional growth, increased performance and personal improvement.

Since 1980, when I was teaching, coaching and working on my advanced degrees, I have been intrigued with the evaluation process of athletes, students, teachers and administrators. I wondered how to accurately measure current performance and improve future performance. How does one incorporate team leaders, managers, the owner and the employee being evaluated into the process?

The system we have developed over the years has evolved into a process we believe to be fair and inclusive. The two-part process of our evaluation system involves a performance evaluation of each employee done by his or her respective managers and myself in December, and a self-evaluation and summative evaluation meeting that I hold with each employee before the new season starts each March.

Using our Job Performance Evaluation form, all employees are evaluated by their peers, supervisors, managers and myself at the end of each work season in December and prior to seasonal lay-offs. After the evaluation process has been completed, I review the results with each employee's division manager. During this meeting we discuss new job titles, promotions, and compensation changes. If necessary, additional training or probationary actions are recommended. I share all evaluation information and observations with each employee in a private meeting prior to seasonal lay-off. Personal goals and job performance objectives are set for the next season.

In March the pre-season summative evaluation meeting is held where each employee has the opportunity to outline a list of contributions he or she made to WRE during the previous season, areas they need to improve, suggestions for company improvements and a summary of their job performances.

Based on the evaluation scores and the self-evaluation, the owner completes the overall employee evaluation, sets goals for the next year and notes comments. After evaluation results are discussed with an employee, the next season's wage is established as are any benefit changes or position changes. Once an evaluation is signed, one copy goes to the employee and one is put on file.

The Job Performance Evaluation form has gone through several revisions over the years, with additional categories being added and the number of evaluators changed. The key to the whole evaluation process, however, is getting managers and team leaders comfortable with the system and experienced in evaluating team members fairly.

Although the point system is fairly straight forward (1=poor, 5=average, 10=excellent), each leader implements scoring with different emphasis. Some feel no one should get a 10, others feel 9 and 10 is acceptable. We have found that having at least three or more evaluators results in a more accurate evaluation by generating an average score. Additionally, I have developed an evaluation scale that categorizes the results:

85+	"Excellent"
75+	"Very Good"
65+	"Good"
55	"Average"
45	"Below Average"
35 or less	"Seek New Employment"

Effective evaluation takes time and acceptance; probably a major reason why comprehensive evaluation systems aren't more prevalent in the horticultural industry. However, I feel that advancement and wage increases need to be tied to an employee's level of accountability, responsibility and demonstrated job performance, not just longevity with the company. In conjunction with an evaluation meeting, the setting of goals for the next season and beyond are essential to effective employee management. One of the reasons we retain employees is because many employees can see their jobs developing into a career. The horticultural industry is a growing, expanding industry with a promising future for WRE, its employees and the southern New England market. At our summary evaluation meeting in March, we mutually agree to goals in performance for the upcoming year and discuss what I call the ISP (Individual Success Plan). We identify the ultimate goal/career position for which an employee would like to strive, the requirements/qualifications needed to attain it, and a plan to gain the necessary certifications, experience and techniques to achieve that goal. It may take one year, three years, or more, but at least the employee has a goal and an outline of the steps required to reach his objective.

I am convinced effective evaluations improve employee performance, but I will confess it is not easy. There have been problems, which have led us to revamp our system from year to year to make it more effective, fair and respected by the employees and managers who must use the program. Central to the evaluation effectiveness is the empowerment and support of the team leaders, managers and directors.

LESSONS LEARNED:

1. The evaluation of team members is an essential tool to improve employee performance, determine appropriate wage increases and promote workers to new positions.
2. All employees involved in the evaluation process must feel it is fair and must feel they have input in the process.
3. Management must be committed to the evaluation process in order for it to be effective.

CHAPTER 14
EMPOWER YOUR TEAM

"Coming together is a beginning; keeping together is progress; working together is success."

Henry Ford II

The most difficult thing for me to do as my business grew was to delegate responsibilities to my team leaders and managers and then get out of their way.

When my business was small and I had only a few employees, it was essential for me to wear many hats: salesman, marketer, scheduler, banker, office manager and worker. However, as the business grew and I assumed additional responsibilities from year to year, the burgeoning workload and daily stress began to take its toll in the workplace and in my personal life. I finally reached the point when drastic changes had to be made for my own survival.

Although it was difficult to relinquish control of certain job functions like estimating, inventory control, scheduling and marketing, these functions are now performed by others more efficiently and more effectively than I could. Additionally, I now have more time to devote to soliciting new business, speaking at horticultural conferences, traveling, coaching my employees, and writing—all the things I enjoy.

Letting go is difficult but the results can be "freeing" for you and your team. The transformation won't occur overnight, and it won't occur without problems, but when you empower your team you raise members' levels of performance and motivation.

My solution to implement a policy of participatory management, where I began to delegate responsibilities and empower managers with decision-making opportunities, was eventually very successful. But as I said, success didn't happen overnight. The first step was to establish the WRE Planning Committee which was formed in 1996 and consisted of key team leaders, designers, managers and me. We met in the winter months (January, February, March) to review our business in terms of what was working and what needed improving, and we set goals for the coming year. Since its inception, the WRE Planning Committee has become a driving force for WRE's growth, development and success.

Our current committee has 15 members including the VP/director of operations, accounting manager, office manager, landscape designer, the managers of our nursery, carpentry, masonry, landscape construction, landscape maintenance and lighting divisions, key team leaders and me.

The committee's three winter meetings are held at a local country club restaurant, a relaxing, pleasant environment away from the office. We review the business in terms of what is (or isn't) working, discuss ways to improve, reinforce our company's mission and outline short- and long-term goals for the future. We update or revise the business plan, employee handbook, and company policies and procedures if necessary. We discuss significant employee problems and arrive at solutions.

Although we have not yet reached our goal, we are on the road towards a culture of complete empowerment and shared management. Team members are now responsible for scheduling, project implementation, problem resolution, and methods to improve the efficiency and profitability of our landscape projects.

The division managers and I support team members with what they need to successfully carry out their jobs. Coaching has become an important function of our managers, who are encouraged to support, motivate, and praise individual and team successes. In order to reach this point, we had to build a team whose members believe in our values, purpose, mission and business philosophy, and who are comfortable in our company culture.

Negative Personalities

Occasionally we hire an employee who doesn't fit our company culture or believe in our values. They either decide to leave or are let go. Negative influences play havoc with team morale, motivation and productivity. The sooner divisive elements are removed, the sooner a team regains its focus, spirit and motivation.

I find it extremely difficult to fire employees and I am careful to take other measures first. But in every instance when an employee who did not support our mission, culture or team spirit has been let go, the positive reaction from remaining team members was remarkable. In addition, the company sends a clear message that we are sincere about fostering a positive company culture and will take the necessary, and sometimes difficult steps, to protect the team from negative influences.

Share Decision-making Powers

Many employees are familiar with a work environment based on the hierarchy of owner and manager at the top, laborers at the bottom. This culture is typically based on a "command and control" management style. Today's workers do not respond well to this type of management philosophy. They want an opportunity to be involved in the decision-making process, to become partners, to determine the success (or failure) of their team. This is the essence of empowerment. Management shares information with team members who are encouraged to provide input. They are self-directed and take on increased responsibilities and accountability as they learn more, grow and succeed.

Today's smart business owners and managers take advantage of the wide range of talents and skills of employees. With coaching and support, empowered employees will not only do their jobs well, but, in most cases, will do it better than the owner or manager could.

I recently read a book titled *"If You Want It Done Right, You Don't Have To Do It Yourself!"* by Donna M. Genett, Ph.D. Genett illustrates that effective delegation results in more work being done better, thereby providing more time for the owner/manager to develop the vision, coach the teams and enjoy a personal life. I can offer several personal testimonials to this from my own business experience:

The WRE Newsletters

One responsibility I enjoyed was the creation of our quarterly newsletter. I developed the layout, written content and visuals myself.
As the business grew and my daily responsibilities increased, however, it became difficult for me to dedicate the time required to create the newsletter on a regular basis. Over time, there were some issues that were never completed. As Lynda Martel began to assume more and more marketing duties, I recognized that the newsletter would have to be handled by her if it was going to get out on time.

Lynda skillfully set up deadlines for content, printing and mailing. She created a format for the newsletter's layout that remained consistent from issue to issue. I would provide her with a list of topics I wanted to include in each newsletter and she developed the stories from there, finding (or taking) photographs to support the message. Once I reviewed the copy, she would arrange for the printing and mailing. As a result, this high-quality newsletter is mailed out regularly and has received numerous accolades from our clients for its professional appearance, writing style and level of information.

It was hard to delegate this task at first, but in retrospect, the change was a good one. I had one less task to think about, giving me more time to do what I do best: solicit new business, sell and manage my valuable staff.

Landscape Lighting Division Sales

In the late '80s, after my landscape business started taking off, I investigated the prospects of adding landscape lighting to the mix. I enrolled in a workshop offered by Nightscaping™, a nationally known landscape lighting brand, and began offering this new service to existing and new clients.

Over time I became fairly proficient at designing and installing lighting systems. It was not a huge part of our business—we averaged five to eight lighting projects each year—but at that pace I was able to sell, design and install them all. In the mid-'90s, as the landscape construction business volume grew, it became more difficult for me to promote and implement all our landscape lighting designs. I had a staff member who could help with installations and maintenance but no one who could handle sales.

Landscape lighting illuminates walkways and patio.

In 1997 we were managing several large landscape construction installations that required lighting. I was stretched to my limit with other responsibilities and could not handle these new lighting projects. Fortunately, I was ordering materials from Major Electric Supply, Inc. through a very capable lighting consultant, Kathy Quinn. Kathy offered to help with the landscape lighting design, product orders, and lighting installations during her free time.

The results of her first major installation on behalf of WRE were wonderful. I knew then that I needed a specialist to oversee and grow our Landscape Lighting Division. In the fall of 1997 I made Kathy an offer, which she accepted, and since then she has steadily guided our lighting division to the point it is at today. Thanks to Kathy's strong sales skills and design talent, we now install landscape lighting in most of our landscape projects. Kathy also maintains the lighting for all our accounts, actively markets our landscape lighting services, addresses groups at garden events and industry trade shows, and is instrumental in helping our company create award-winning landscapes.

Trusting Kathy to deal with my clients on a one-to-one basis was not an easy task for me. Our sales styles were very different in the beginning, but over time she adapted a bit and I relaxed a bit, and we created a formula for success. Kathy now handles our lighting designs in a way I have neither the time nor the talent to do. Best of all, the Landscape Lighting Division continues to grow each year. Kathy is as proud of this division as I am, and handles it with focus, attention, and care.

LESSONS LEARNED:

1. Sharing decision-making responsibilities empowers your managers and team leaders.
2. The more work an owner can delegate to responsible managers and team leaders, the more efficient and effective day-to-day operations become.
3. A planning committee with key management provides a forum to discuss and resolve problems and make improvements to the business. This committee is a driving force to the company's growth, development and success.
4. Adopt a leadership style with which you are comfortable. Coaching, delegating and support fit the needs of today's work force.
5. Once you have delegated responsibilities, get out of the way!

CHAPTER 15
CONTINUE TO LEARN—AND ADVANCE

"Education is no longer thought of as a preparation for adult life, but as a continuing process of growth and development from birth until death."

Stephen Mitchell

My educational training at the University of Rhode Island and nine years of experience teaching students biology and coaching athletes at Killingly High School in Danielson, Conn. helped fortify my respect for continuing education, and showed me the value of teaching and training in improving performance. I have instilled this philosophy in my business and although I invest heavily in new tools, equipment and vehicles, continuing education for all team members is paramount.

Beginning with the specific skills required to do each job, my goal is to offer every employee willing to learn an opportunity to advance his career. Acquiring horticultural certification and certain licenses are integral to this advancement, as well as obtaining management, computer, team-building and communication skills. I have always exercised a policy of reimbursing employees for expenses related to continuing education as long as the courses or classes are directly related to their horticultural advancement plans.

As mentioned in Chapter 12, we encourage team members to gain official recognition from organizations that certify RI Horticulturalists, the LVLIA (Low Voltage Lighting Institute of America) for lighting design certification, Landscape Architecture Certification, NOFA's Organic Land Care Accreditation, and the Connecticut and Rhode Island Pesticide Applicators licenses, among others.

Many of these certificates can be obtained by attending classes like those offered by the University of Rhode Island's Cooperative Extension, RINLA, the RI Department of Motor Vehicles, New England Grows (a local trade show), NOFA and other local educational programs.

Periodically, I offer in-house seminars for staff members on plant identification, pruning, landscape lighting, landscape project estimating, the construction of stone walls or water features, and more.

For three years, Lynda Martel, Ken Mazur and I ran a two-day workshop called GEM (Growth, Effectiveness, Management) for small business owners. Our classes focused on branding, marketing and advertising, improving the efficiency of the business operation via computer technology and software products, estimating and pricing, hiring and retaining employees, and managing for success.

Last year I arranged a wellness session for employees interested in better nutrition. I have also signed up employees for one-on-one classes to improve their management skills, counsel them with personal problems, or help them deal with life-threatening issues such as alcohol abuse.

Two years ago, we brought in Dr. Bob Cohen, a professional therapist and business coach, to conduct a team-building workshop on the first day of our new season. We experienced very good results. The next year, we invited Bob back to run a communications workshop designed to help us improve our skills in relaying important information to other members of the team. As we identify educational needs, new workshops will be scheduled—an important process in making WRE a better place to work, grow and enjoy.

Why the investment in educational opportunities? What's the payback? Here's a list of benefits, many of which directly affect profitability:

• By attending industry trade shows, seminars and conferences, employees learn about new techniques and products to help improve skills and do a better job. This has a direct effect on the bottom line.

• Trade shows, seminars and conferences also give employees an opportunity to network with other attendees, vendors and speakers. Valuable relationships develop and provide opportunities for feedback and advice in "real world" situations. This can have a positive effect on an employee's self-esteem and professional image.

• As employees obtain licenses and certifications, they improve themselves and become more valuable to the company. The more employees learn and grow, the greater the rewards to them and the firm.

• Employees who are given the opportunity to advance their careers create long-term relationships with your company. It is far less expensive to retain and reward a loyal employee than it is to hire and train new ones.

• Happy, motivated, educated employees behave and perform in a more professional manner, leading to higher customer satisfaction. Satisfied customers will not only hire your firm again and again, they will refer your firm to others over and over.

• As a company grows and leadership positions open up, management can recruit qualified, professional employees from its own staff.

LESSONS LEARNED:

1. Investing in employees' continuing education helps them improve professional skills, advance careers and enhance their value to the company.
2. Industry events are important for employees who benefit from advancing their educations, learning about new products and services, and networking with other professionals in their field.
3. Long-term employee relationships are the result of a company that advocates and provides additional training.
4. Employees who continue to learn will do their jobs better and help improve customer satisfaction.
5. Educated employees become a valuable resource and enable the business to fill new leadership positions.

CHAPTER 16
BECOME THE EXPERT

"Leaders give more to volunteer organizations and leaders get more from volunteer organizations in personal satisfaction and contacts that can be leveraged into other opportunities."

General Michaelson (Sun Tzu)

Since the first days of opening my business, I have been involved in many trade organizations: The Rhode Island Christmas Tree Growers Association (RICTGA), The New England Christmas Tree Alliance (NECTA), the Rhode Island Nursery and Landscape Association (RINLA), the National Christmas Tree Association (NCTA) and, most recently, the Master Gardener Foundation of Rhode Island, Inc.

I became involved in these organizations to learn more about issues affecting our industry such as new market trends, new products and new sales techniques. I also got involved to network with speakers, members and vendors—all so I could stay abreast of the latest developments in my field and maintain the highest degree of customer satisfaction through a job well done.

Being a member of an organization is important, but, taking on a leadership position within that organization has been even more rewarding to me. (I always limit active involvement to just several groups, so I can focus my time and energy in more productive ways.) For nine years, I served as chairman of NECTA, and for four years I was chairman of RINLA's education committee—two leadership appointments I thoroughly enjoyed.

While I was chairman of the education committee, our group was able to upgrade the topics and speakers at RINLA's annual winter education seminar, increase attendance, and raise the professional nature of the well-attended event. As an added benefit, I contacted and met outstanding horticultural speakers from all over the United States.

WRE has also been a regular participant in RINLA's Landscape Excellence Design Awards program that was established in 1996 to recognize RINLA members for excellence in residential and commercial landscape design, installation and maintenance, garden features, and public landscape projects. Entering the award competition has been a high priority for WRE since the program first began. We have had the good fortune to win 17 awards, thanks to talented, dedicated employees, and clients who gave us the opportunity to beautify their landscapes.

Another organization I volunteered many years of service to was NECTA. I was elected chairman in 1992 and served in that role for nine of the 11 following years. Our group accomplished many things during that time, including the exchange of state association newsletters, the coordination of New England association meetings, support for the Big E Christmas Tree Contest and Exhibit in Springfield, Mass. and the creation of the NECTA newsletter.

I was also the NECTA conference chairman from 1992 to 2003, and our group organized and promoted NECTA's biennial Christmas Tree Conference, held in Nashua, N.H. from 1993 to 2003. This two-day event attracted outstanding speakers and growers from all over the United States. They presented topics pertinent to Christmas tree growers, retailers and choose-and-cut operations. Besides the knowledge I gained from the conference speakers, the network of friends I made from all types of Christmas tree businesses across the United States. was invaluable to the development of WRE.

If you want to advance your business, it is vital that you become involved in industry trade organizations, particularly in leadership positions. Extended involvement helps you become an expert in your field.

Share Your Knowledge

Becoming a public speaker in your industry can demonstrate your knowledge on a particular topic and increase your professional visibility. Be aware, however, that this is not a comfortable activity for many people. Surveys show that people's two top fears are dying and public speaking. If talking in front of a group makes you uncomfortable, take a public speaking course and then practice with small groups. With extensive preparation, experience and relaxation techniques, you will soon become a confident

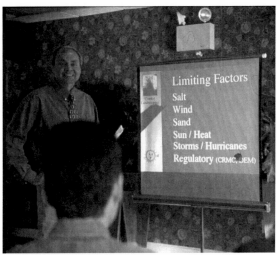

Lecturing to interested groups demonstrates your expertise in your field.

speaker. Practice makes perfect and this talent can generate great exposure for you and your company's brand name.

I can still remember my first speaking appearance. I was in Grade 8 and student council president at Central Junior High School in Bedford, Texas. I was extremely nervous as I struggled to get the attention of 800 students attending a pep rally. The principal finally had to come to the microphone and quiet the boisterous audience so I could proceed. I never forgot that experience, and I worked diligently after that to improve my presence, my speech and my preparation for presentations.

Forty years later, I welcome opportunities to present horticultural PowerPoint® presentations to garden clubs, conduct educational seminars and workshops at the local university, speak to attendees of the Rhode Island Spring Flower and Garden Show, address audiences at industry conferences and seminars, and film short segments aired throughout the state on NBC Channel 10's popular gardening segment "Plant Pro." My public speaking experiences throughout the United States. allow me to indulge my true passion as a teacher, sharing my knowledge in hopes it will help others.

LESSONS LEARNED:

1. Assuming leadership positions in trade organizations benefits your company by exposing you to new trends and new product information, and offering networking opportunities with other professionals. These help you stay ahead of the curve in your industry.
2. Public speaking is a great opportunity to create awareness for your company and yourself among your peers. And it can be fun!
3. You get far more out of efforts as a volunteer in terms of personal satisfaction, knowledge, new friends and colleagues than you put in.

CHAPTER 17
EMBRACE TECHNOLOGY

"View information technology as an opportunity to simplify, streamline and improve your business processes."

Ken Mazur

In 1993 the computer used by my office manager to type letters and do basic accounting died. Although I did not personally use the computer (I was computer illiterate), I had hoped to put our written mailing list on it to see if we could print labels instead of handwriting several thousands of them for mailings—a tiresome process at best.

Fortunately for WRE and me, The Computer Lab, a local computer retailer and service center, sent Ken Mazur to our office. Ken not only solved our immediate problem, but, over the next 12 years, helped me grow my business by reorganizing the way I did things, helped us look more professional, and eventually assumed the role of systems manager and friend.

We now use computers for many tasks: four PCs are used for accounting; nine Macs are used for our customer database and product inventory, pricing, catalog and label-making, word processing, email, the creation of our quarterly newsletters, job estimating and job costing, digital scans, data storage, presentations and spreadsheets. We have also acquired two scanners, three laser printers and four ink-jet printers, one photo printer, two digital cameras and one presentation projector. Our computers "talk" to each other thanks to an ethernet and fiber-optic network, and we research information and download files with a high-speed Internet connection. We create jazzy presentations in PowerPoint and manage our customer database and product inventory with FileMaker Pro®.

How has all this technology benefited my business? Three major ways: our daily business operations have been streamlined and we operate more efficiently; our brand image has been enhanced to make us more professional; and we are more profitable.

Streamlining Operations

Take a look at your business and determine how many tasks are repetitive: customer mailings, label creation, job estimates, product pricing and product inventory. How many of these tasks do you do manually? How do you check the status of a project? How do you find an address, phone number or retrieve and distribute driving directions? How many staff members need the same information on a daily basis? Technology automates repetitive tasks, keeps running records for accuracy and knowledge sharing, provides your team with valuable, up-to-date information in a matter of seconds, and reduces errors with software products that take the guesswork out of calculations. Technology saves you time and money.

Enhancing Brand Image

We use graphic software products such QuarkXpress® and PhotoShop to create many vehicles that enhance our professional image. Formatted templates are used to generate invoices, estimates, letters, newsletters, and flyers with our brand identity. Preferred type fonts and attractive layouts present a unified, consistent appearance. Digital cameras and printers generate "before" and "after" photos of a client's site and are used to support project estimates, communicate work in progress, and expedite final billing and payment. We create and publish multipage, full-color newsletters in-house. Our Web site promotes our spectrum of products and services to current and potential customers, and provides them with valuable information on plant care and landscape design. PowerPoint software allows me to create dynamic lectures that enforce my company's professional image when communicating information to various groups and organizations. There is no end to the software products and technology available on the market to help small companies look and act more professional. We do not take advantage of all the technology available, but we are committed to advancing with the times. A company that looks professional has a competitive edge when it comes to attracting a certain level of clientele.

Increased Profits

Computer technology allows WRE to access information and respond to clients faster, monitor inventory better to keep popular items in stock, estimate jobs more accurately to minimize the loss of profits, and create an appealing, consistent, professional image for our communications materials. All these things add up to greater productivity and efficiency, higher profit margins and increased customer satisfaction.

It is interesting to note that computers are one of the few capital investments we have made that have consistently increased in quality, speed and function, while the price each year goes down! As technology continues to advance, yearly upgrades in software and the replacement of existing computers have become part of our business plan.

Since this technological transformation didn't take place overnight, how was it implemented? And, knowing that the owner isn't a computer wizard, who embraced the system and actually used the computers?

At first it was Ken who focused on the high payoff tasks and eliminated information or production bottlenecks. But as our company embraced technology, other employees began to use their computers and software products to streamline tasks and make their specific job functions easier.

Cost Estimates

Several years ago, Mark Grenier, our vice president and director of operations, spent the winter at home recovering from Lyme disease. During that time he used his iMac® and Excel software to create an estimating and job-costing template for our landscape construction projects. Using a cost/overhead/profit formula and a retail formula I have used over the years, Mark created a template that incorporates calculations to cost out materials, equipment, vehicles and labor, along with allocated overhead percentages and a profit computation. As we input the amount of materials, plants, equipment, vehicle hours and labor hours required to complete the job, the template automatically calculates an estimate with profit percentages in a matter of seconds.

Mark later developed a second template that converts materials, plants, equipment, vehicles and labor costs directly into a retail estimate—which we traditionally had used—based on a cost/overhead formula. The final estimated cost is generated automatically, falling between the cost/overhead/profit method and the retail method.

In addition, the estimate template has a job-costing component where actual costs can be entered to determine our true profit margin on each job. Team leaders receive a duplicate sheet (minus retail prices), which serves as a guideline for the amount of materials, equipment, vehicle hours, and most importantly, labor hours budgeted for the job.

Since Mark developed this program, the time it takes to create a project estimate has been reduced by 75 percent. What used to take me hours (or days) by hand is now complete in minutes. This eases what used to be a huge bottleneck. And with a budget to guide them, our team leaders do a better job of keeping costs down on every project they install.

Product Inventory and Pricing

Keeping track of our plant inventory, creating labels, establishing prices and organizing customer orders were tasks never done accurately or efficiently by hand.

Ken Mazur, Lynda Martel and Gina Detorio attacked this problem, and over a year's time created an inventory database in FileMaker Pro.

We created a standardized pricing formula with "Pfactors" (profit factors) that automatically calculates a certain percentage above wholesale costs to generate retail prices. The inventory program also allows us to generate plant labels that list each plant's Latin name, common name, size, price and the name of the client who purchased the plants, all in a matter of minutes. Gina, our nursery manager, now enters each new order into the database, prints out labels and tags all incoming plants within minutes after they arrive at the nursery. This job previously took days to do by hand.

The inventory team also developed a customer picking ticket for landscape plans. The "tickets" list all designer-specified plants organized by location at the site, Latin name, quantity, size and price. Mark and I use picking tickets to create project estimates, and project team leaders use them as guides to ensure that all the plants in the design arrive at the job site. If a plant dies, Gina can pull up the plant list and order a replacement for our clients instantly. Once a job is complete, the final picking ticket with the total plants actually installed generates a sales ticket for the final bill. As the sales slip is generated, the plants are removed from our inventory, giving us greater awareness and control over the number of plants in stock.

By printing out our entire inventory we also generate a product catalog we use for reference when a client calls for the availability or price of a plant. Without this catalog it took days to physically walk the property to research our inventory, look up the correct prices, and call the customer back. (Not the way to exceed a customer's expectations!)

Billing

Computer technology has also helped us tackle the biggest frustration for the office staff, the clients, and me: billing. As our business grew, accurate and regular monthly billing was essential for generating the cash flow we needed to meet monthly expenses. Initially, I controlled all the billing, which, over time, proved to be a huge bottleneck.

Again, using Excel, Mark Grenier streamlined the billing process by creating job report templates that could later be converted into bills. Our office manager, Kristen Grieco, enters the bills into our QuickBooks accounting program, and, after I review and approve them, prints the final bills on our letterhead. Eventually, we streamlined this process even further and job reports now go directly to Kristen who converts them into bills in QuickBooks and runs off copies for me to examine and sign.

To ensure accuracy of input, Kristen makes sure team leaders and managers fill out their job reports with information that is thorough, accurate and clear. Since I removed myself from the billing process, it is now done much quicker, smoother and it goes out on time every month.

Accounting

Jane Perry, our accounting manager since 1993, has witnessed the ups and downs of our landscape business as well as our tremendous growth over the years. To keep up with that growth, we had to acquire an accounting program that could provide the financial data we needed, be compatible with our accounting firm's software, and be accessible to Mark, Kristen, Jane and me over the network.

We purchased four PCs to run the QuickBooks software that manages all our accounting functions. QuickBooks provides us with valuable, "real-time" information we can use to improve company operations, develop and monitor budgets, and regularly evaluate our financial condition.

Jane produces weekly reports that detail our accounts receivables, accounts payables and forecasted cash-flow requirements. She also produces monthly P&L statements and balance sheets, prints checks, generates budgets including employee compensation reports, vehicle and equipment costs, sales by customer or amount, and monthly revenue figures. This financial information helps us make educated decisions when we need to purchase equipment, hire additional employees, or buy plants and materials on sale.

We've come a long way since purchasing that first computer from Ken. Since then, he has taken on the role of systems manager, stopping in twice a week to deal with systems problems, supervise back-ups, provide updates, and redefine ways we use our current computers and software.

But most important, Ken helps me look at my business differently, defines ways to become more efficient and profitable, and provides the support and knowledge I need to understand and incorporate computer technology into daily business operations. Thanks to Ken, I now recognize the value of computers and with his support, and my innovative staff, our business continues to devise new uses and applications for technology, making us more efficient and professional.

> *LESSONS LEARNED:*
>
> *1. Computer technology can improve the efficiency, accuracy and effectiveness of many tasks, and it helps your company look more professional.*
> *2. By improving the efficiency and accuracy with which jobs are performed, your company benefits from increased productivity and profits.*
> *3. Anyone can learn how to use a computer. All it takes is time and practice.*

CHAPTER 18

DON'T LOSE YOUR WAY

"By experience, we find out a short way by a long wandering."

Roger Ascham

Since beginning WRE, I have experimented with several diverse business ventures including the GEM Business Seminars, GolfScapes, Christmas tree and holiday retail sales, a mail-a-wreath program, and agri-entertainment events such as the Spooky Halloween, Festival of Lights and Western hayrides. Not all of these ventures were successful, but they did help me develop five main tenets that any new service must now meet before we introduce it as part of the company. To explain how these tenets came to be, let me briefly trace the history of our agri-entertainment and Christmas business experiences.

Christmas Tree Business: 1972-2002

WRE was founded in 1972 with the unceremonious planting of 2,000 evergreen transplants expected to generate future Christmas tree sales. The "future," when it comes to Christmas trees, arrives in around six to eight years—the time it takes a seedling tree to mature to a 7-foot saleable size. To generate sales more quickly, we also dug and burlapped live trees for landscape plantings.

1978 marked our first selling season as harvesting from our own fields began. Each year sales improved as we added special features like Santa, a Christmas retail shop, wreaths, a nationwide mail-a-wreath shipping program, hayrides and live B&B (balled and burlapped) Christmas trees.

Most noteworthy was that we were the only Christmas tree operation in New England to offer trees shaken free of debris and with fresh cuts on the tree butt for better water absorption. We baled trees in a mesh net for easier handling, installed some trees in a patented 4-brace tree stand, and offered home delivery, all free of charge. Business grew rapidly and by 1989 we were selling over 1,200 trees a season and generating over $115,000 in gross sales. Membership in the RICTGA and NECTA organizations and my tenure as their respective president and chairman helped us learn more about raising and marketing trees.

In the 1990s, increased competition in our market and nationwide began to affect sales. When I first opened we had 10 competitors within a 15-

mile radius. Over time, that increased to over 25 competitors, including the noted price-busters Wal-Mart and Home Depot. Retail prices of cut trees began a slow but steady downward spiral.

Without my own inventory of live trees to offer choose-and-cut customers, I had to purchase trees wholesale, which reduced profit margins. In addition, the vagaries of southern New England weather resulted in a short, four-week sales season from Thanksgiving to Christmas. Severe weather often reduced traffic and sales dramatically.

As the 1990s came to an end, so did our Christmas business. Though steeped in tradition and supported by a core of loyal customers—one customer had been coming with his family for over 25 years—we began losing money each season and sales were reduced to an average of 500 trees. Further eroding our profits were labor costs. To extend the work season for our landscape employees, we used many of them to help with retail sales. Unfortunately, their pay rates were much higher than the Christmas tree business could afford.

After five unprofitable seasons, it became painfully obvious that we were losing money when we could least afford to—just before entering our lean winter months. In 2003 we made the difficult decision to close down the Christmas business.

Tradition is an extremely powerful motivator and it was difficult to abandon the origins of Wood River Evergreens, but our very survival was at stake. We made the decision to focus on our core and very profitable landscape design, construction and maintenance business divisions.

Landscaper By Day, Dracula By Night

In 1991 we were in the middle of a severe recession: the economy was down, the stock market was suffering, and our gross sales had dropped 50 percent from 1989. Our immediate sales goals were to attract new customers, grow revenue from existing customers, and explore ways to earn supplemental income with our existing resources, which included 12 acres of land, four acres of evergreen trees, a tractor, several nursery wagons, and our crew of talented employees including Lianne Maher, an accomplished actress, singer, teacher and all-around creative individual.

Lianne and I put our heads together and discussed using the property for seasonal hayrides, an agri-entertainment endeavor becoming popular with farm-based retail businesses. Although neither of us had been on a Halloween hayride, our initial discussion sparked Lianne's creative talents and within a few days she returned with ideas for a hayride route, the scenes, a list of items we would need to produce the event, their costs, and the recommendation that we could pull a hayride together in time for Halloween that October.

From our first season in 1991 when Wood River Evergreens' "Spooky Halloween Hayride" ran for five nights and attracted 1,500 customers, our humble event blossomed into southern New England's premiere Halloween hayride, recognized by many as the best Halloween event for the whole family. Our hayride attracted between 8,500 to 9,500 visitors each October, before ending in 2000.

Lianne put us all to work—including me. Each October night I dressed up as Dracula to drive a tractor that pulled a caravan of three wagons. On each run the wagons carried approximately 100 patrons who shrieked with delight as we wound our way through the creepy exhibits situated among the trees throughout the moonlit fields. Other WRE employees were paid to escort the wagons, park cars, perform as actors, sell retail tickets, or book rides and answer telephones.

Frank as Dracula with Lianne Maher as Morticia.

At its height, Lianne (director) and Mark Grenier (assistant director and sound technician) created many elaborate productions—some with over 35 actors, 15 support personnel and 18 choreographed scenes. There were custom-created sound tracks, costumes, masks, elaborate sets and special lighting effects. Over the 10 years the hayride was in business, "Dracula" made more than 800 runs through the property, entertaining over 65,000 delighted adults and children.

Those of us involved in the hayride started work at the end of each 8- or 10-hour day of landscaping, often ending our long days at midnight, only to get up the following day for 6 a.m. start-time.

As the event grew more successful, the demands on the commitment of land, equipment and personnel increased as well. Many of us were working 16 to 18 hours per day in October, and the demands soon took a toll on our employees and on our core business. Eventually more farms and business owners created Halloween hayride events, a lawsuit scare highlighted the tremendous liability of having so many people on our property at night, employees were being worn out, and our profits weren't justifying our investments in the event.

Mark and I made a commitment to operate the event for at least 10 years in honor of Lianne who died unexpectedly in May of 1998. The year 2000 marked that anniversary, and, after some deliberation, everyone agreed that Wood River Evergreens' Spooky Halloween Hayride event had run its course. It was time to shut down the event.

To continue to celebrate our affection for Lianne, we now run the Lianne Maher Memorial Scholarship Golf Tournament at the beautiful Richmond Country Club nearby, and we have raised thousands of dollars which is awarded annually to one graduate from Chariho and Westerly High schools in support of a college major in education, music or horticulture. To date, eight students have received $1,000 scholarships—a fitting memorial to Lianne.

Although the Spooky Halloween Hayride closed in 2000, former hayride customers still remind us of how much they miss the event. This makes all associated with the event proud to have been involved.

Besides the lingering good will, the event also exposed our landscaping services to thousands of potential customers. One of the most extensive landscape projects we have completed to date was the direct result of the hayride.

Over the years, we experimented with other hayrides: The Festival of Lights Hayride (December 1992-1995), and a short-lived summer Western Hayride (1994). Small numbers of attendees drove the costs for these two events way above what they generated in sales.

I have no regrets for these agri-entertainment experiments: we brought happiness, joy and fun to thousands of customers, who even today remember the great times they had on our hayrides and the beautiful, real Christmas trees they purchased every year. Our experiences made it clear, however, that we were not entertainers and we needed to stay focused on our core landscaping business. As a result, I have adopted five tenets that guide me when considering the addition of any new business ventures in the future.

1. Remain true to the core business. WRE is a comprehensive landscape design, construction and maintenance firm. By staying true to its core, we can continue to improve customer service by providing skilled, talented and trained personnel to support customer needs.

2. Expand the core with complementary services that the client needs and that you can do well. For us, that means services such as masonry, carpentry, landscape lighting and water features. These are services we can perform with excellence, current team members and profitably.

3. Offer services you can perform in-house. Unlike subcontracted services, performing tasks with an in-house staff allows you to retain control over the timing, quality and completion of the service. Completing projects on time and under budget, along with client satisfaction, is greatly enhanced.

4. Subcontract any service you cannot complete with excellence and a profit. Hire only those subcontractors who meet your standards for quality and service.

5. Educate the consumer about the new services whenever and wherever possible. We do this not only to promote a new service, but to educate customers on how these new services will benefit them: irrigation systems to conserve water, landscape lighting to make walkways safer, organic lawn treatments for the environment, and so on.

By following these tenets, we have successfully expanded services to include landscape lighting, masonry, water features and carpentry.

Landscape lighting is a perfect fit with our business. Every landscape can benefit from the safety afforded by and the beauty of subtle illumination. In 1997 we hired lighting designer Kathy Quinn to manage a new landscaping lighting division and our landscape designers now spec landscape lighting into each plan drawn up. Our clients can either "set up" their site for lighting in the future, or install lighting with the final design.

Masonry services are also a perfect fit with our business. In the past, finding reliable subcontractors for masonry projects was always a challenge; none of the available subs could meet our demanding schedules, desired level of quality and detail, or stay on the project until it was completed.

Five years ago, I hired our own crew of stonemasons. In addition to my ability to schedule masonry work with confidence that it will be completed on time, the quality of their work has gained a positive reputation in our market, generated awards and attracted new clients.

Wooden landscape elements such as arbors, pergolas, trellises and decks were also difficult to get completed by subcontractors on time and to our clients' specifications. Since 1994, I have had carpenters on staff who create high-quality, custom, wooden structures for our customers. Two years ago, we built a heated carpentry shop, allowing us to extend the season for custom-carpentry work into the winter months.

All of these supplemental services have enhanced our landscape projects and generated additional income without compromising the quality of our services or customer satisfaction.

Some subcontractor relationships can be very successful if their product quality and customer service is in line with your ideals. We work with several top-notch subcontractors: Fred Burns of Tree Works Unlimited handles all our clients' large tree-care and removal needs; Leo Beausoleil handles all our driveway paving projects; and Peter Reusch has done all our excavating since 1986. Steve Gowen, Shoreline Lawn Sprinklers, Inc. installs and maintains all our irrigation systems; Tom Fuimarello, Traveling Trees, handles all our large tree transplanting; Bill Gordon handles our trucking needs; and Joe Morrone, Morrone Trucking, provides loam and supplies.

Adding services to our company's mix has taught me some valuable lessons. Today, we analyze any potential service to determine if it meets our clients' needs, complements our current line of offerings, meets our standards for quality and timing, and adds to the bottom line. When adding a service isn't a good fit, we hire dependable subcontractors to provide the service for us as long as their dedication to quality and service mirrors ours. When that happens, we all win: the client, WRE and the subcontracting firm.

LESSONS LEARNED:

1. Focus on your core business.
2. New business ventures that detract from the core in terms of personnel, finances, equipment, etc., could undermine the success of the new division and jeopardize your business.
3. Every new business venture should fit the needs of your clients, meet their standards of quality, fit the talents and abilities of your employees, and be done profitably.

CHAPTER 19
BECOME THE "SERVING" LEADER

"The main job of a leader is to help his and her people succeed in accomplishing their goals. And when people accomplish their goals and win, everybody wins."

Ken Blanchard - "The Heart of a Leader"

I have always been fascinated with great leaders and their unique leadership styles, strengths, and resiliency in the face of defeat.

No one exemplifies these characteristics to me more than Winston Churchill. Criticized and ridiculed by countless British politicians prior to 1940, his "radical views" were eventually embraced. He was elected prime minister, and experienced his finest hour as a wartime leader in the defeat of Nazi Germany only to be defeated at the polls following the conclusion of World War II.

Like all great leaders, Churchill articulated his goals and philosophies in a compelling and moving manner, recognized the value of relationships, and exhibited a leadership style that was predicated on responsibility, optimism, decisiveness and clear direction. He also displayed the secret of all great leaders: they serve their constituents.

I have held a variety of leadership positions during my lifetime: student council president, football captain, biology teacher, head coach of a cross country and track team, association president, chairman and committee chairman, worshipful master of Charity Lodge, and president of my own firm.

In spite of all this experience, however, I often felt uncomfortable serving as the "boss" of my growing staff. The mounting responsibilities of managing and directing the business, as well as hiring, training and disciplining workers caused me great frustration, anguish and considerable stress. It often became obvious that the staff wasn't real happy with my style or behavior either.

Ken Blanchard, Patricia Zigarini and Drea Zigarini, authors of *"Leadership and the One Minute Manager,"* detail the effectiveness of situational leadership—directing, coaching, supporting and delegating—when used with the appropriate developmental level of teammates.

Charles Vander Kooi, a noted motivational speaker, once remarked that today's workers do not respond well to the "command and control" leadership style used by the armed forces after WWII and adopted by businesses in the 1950s.

When I listened to a Vander Kooi presentation, I realized my leadership style was a problem for my workers—and for me! None of us liked a style of giving orders to be followed without question and handing out punishment when the orders were not followed. Further, my years of coaching experience left me with a natural leadership style that fit my personality better—and the personalities of my talented, experienced and self-motivated employees as well.

I preferred directing, planning, monitoring progress, praising and supporting my employees with what they needed for success. The wisdom of this leadership style was demonstrated years earlier when the high school track team I coached won numerous titles. I changed my leadership style at work, began delegating responsibilities, and invited my staff to share in the day-to-day decision-making process; simple steps that had a profound effect on everyone in the company, including me.

I would like to say the transition between styles was smooth and perfect, but it wasn't. Although I let my managers assign crew members and vehicles each day, I retained control over project scheduling. Because I had a tendency to change project scheduling, often as a knee-jerk reaction to last-minute client demands, my actions created problems. My managers were unable to finish jobs because crews would be pulled off a project to support my new scheduling needs; the crews' enthusiasm was eroded when they left projects unfinished time and again; and the inefficiencies in time affected our bottom line.

Delegate Responsibilities

Eventually, reluctantly, and nervously in 2003, I removed myself from the daily scheduling of projects, and like magic the system became more organized and more efficient than I could have imagined.

Mark Grenier, VP/director of operations, created templates for scheduling projects, personnel and equipment. At the end of each day, Mark now reviews each on-going project with team leaders, updates the scheduling worksheet, and is ready the following morning with assignments for the next day's activities—subject only to minor modifications.

Now, all projects are scheduled through Mark. He calls clients to let them know what day they can expect our crews to be there. He can comfortably convey a change in the schedule with little fear of a client's complaint because they now are given information that will help them plan accordingly in advance.

With me out of the process, scheduling runs much smoother. As I delegated more day-to-day responsibilities to my staff, I found more time to do the things I enjoy, and the tasks they now handle are completed in a more professional, more efficient and more timely fashion.

This emphasizes an important point: for any leadership style to be effective, you need the right people in the right role.

Over the years, hiring and retaining key personnel, training team members and shifting people to roles they enjoy has been a priority of mine. I make sure that everyone understands their value and the effect their roles have on the success of our company. It is important to extend praise, recognition and rewards for my employees' efforts to let them know they are appreciated. Mark Twain once said, "I can live for two months on a good compliment." Praise is an important component of successful leadership. You will be amazed at the effect that thoughtful, appreciative remarks can have.

In *"The Serving Leader,"* Ken Jennings and John Stahlwert write about "upending the pyramid." The organization chart of a traditional business typically consists of leaders at the top, followed by managers, team leaders, staff and finally customers, in descending order. To be a true "serving" leader, the pyramid needs to be inverted.

Because this is a vastly different model, some of my staff are still learning how this works. If asked, some team members will say they work for the owner and support their supervisors. What I remind them—and show by example—is that we ALL work for the customer, and it is my job to train, motivate, support and assist employees so they can serve clients better.

Positive Attitude = Positive Results

It took me a while to realize just how my moods, problem-solving techniques and communication style affected staff morale. When I was angry, short-tempered, or relaying bad news about current projects or my concerns about our financial status, I was lowering the morale and motivation of my staff. Conversely, as I learned to be calm (in the face of difficulties), friendly, supportive, appreciative and careful with my selection of words, the morale of my staff got better, the working atmosphere improved and motivation levels were raised. This may not be a surprising discovery, but it's an important one that I apply to my daily actions.

These results illustrate the "Hawthorne Effect"; people who believe good, positive things are happening are motivated to do better. However, the more you believe things are getting worse, the lower your motivation will be to improve.

Foremost, a leader has to articulate a vision of the future, assemble a capable team to carry out the vision and work passionately to see it implemented.

By embracing the idea of being "in service" to others, the steps required to achieve the vision can be taken. Creating and nurturing the relationships between the customer, team members and the leader is key to bringing visions into reality.

LESSONS LEARNED:

1. Successful leaders "serve" their constituents, express their visions in a clear and articulate manner, and lead in a fashion that motivates and inspires.
2. The "coaching and supporting" leadership style is more conducive to today's workforce than the "command and control" style used after WWII.
3. By delegating responsibilities, leaders have more time to focus on their vision, coach and inspire the team, and develop new business.
4. Be calm when dealing with problems; be upbeat when reviewing daily work conditions; and be careful in your choice of words when communicating with others.

CHAPTER 20
USE INTEGRITY AS YOUR COMPASS

"Integrity is one of several paths; it distinguishes itself from the others because it is the right path, and the only one upon which you will never get lost."

M. H. McKee

A true measure of a person's character and personal values is when he (or she) lives with integrity; that is, doing what is right all the time. John C. Maxwell points out that great leaders win the hearts of their followers by showing commitment and consistency, and acting with integrity. In *"The Six Fundamentals of Success,"* Stuart R. Levine notes that conducting yourself and your business with integrity strengthens your brand.

I know this to be true. The credibility I have gained since I first opened Wood River Evergreens has transformed our brand into a well-respected, trusted and recognized name in our market. In today's competitive market, a trusted brand is a powerful asset. But I also know that the positive reputation associated with our brand name can be ruined overnight. Everyone at WRE strives to maintain our values and high standards every day. We aim to act consistently with our values: integrity, tolerance, generosity, fairness and respect. This helps us make good choices—the right choices.

Showing Respect

You will find it difficult to serve and help others unless you respect yourself. I try hard to build up each team member's self-esteem, self-respect and respect for his or her position at WRE and the job he or she performs. I do not tolerate disrespect of themselves, their teammates, managers or clients.

Employees show respect for each other by showing up on time, being courteous, giving their undivided attention when communicating and being active listeners. When problems of disrespect arise, I call the person aside to remind him of his mistakes and point out a better path.

Accountability

Doing what you say you will, honoring your agreements, and being accountable for your actions and performance, makes you reliable, trustworthy and dependable. As a result, your good reputation will grow and prosper.

Many times WRE picks up new clients because competitors do not return phone calls, miss appointments, start but do not finish a job, and refuse to be accountable for lack of performance. This lesson drives the high standards we apply within our company as well as our choices of subcontractors; accountability is the key to client satisfaction.

One of our best clients paid us a high compliment recently. He said we were the most accountable company he ever dealt with; always operating with integrity, always reliable and trustworthy, and always accomplishing what we promised we would on time. In short, we always exceed his expectations. These types of compliments humble me. I am honored when clients recognize our talented and dedicated team members who strive for excellence with every landscape project they install. WRE has rarely missed an agreed-upon deadline for a landscape project—a feat that motivates us to strive even harder.

I wish every client and project resulted in a glowing review, but that isn't the case. To keep on top of our customers' level of satisfaction, we send out customer satisfaction survey cards. By reviewing customers' responses, we can discover gaps in service and project delivery and make necessary improvements.

I look at the survey card as our company's report card: we compare the rankings from year to year and set a goal of improving our average for the next year. The card also serves as a motivational tool to encourage better performance and a renewed dedication to exceed clients' expectations.

Don't "Over Promise"

Inherent in my philosophy, values and way of doing business is the desire to always be honest with the client and strive never to promise more than we can deliver. It is better to do what we promise and exceed expectations than not to accomplish all that was agreed upon and disappoint them.

From the initial client meeting through the design process, construction phase, maintenance and follow-up, it is imperative to communicate frequently and clearly so that everyone is aware of project goals, procedures, potential pitfalls and expectation of the final results. Our teams are taught to communicate daily with clients, solicit feedback, and update clients frequently on the project's progress, future steps and any potential problems. No project goes perfectly, but clear channels of communication help us navigate inherent bumps in the road with minimal impact on the end product.

LESSONS LEARNED:

1. A reputation for integrity is an invaluable asset to a company.
2. Respecting yourself, your employees, your clients and your vendors helps you serve others in a more professional manner.
3. Keeping your agreements will separate you from many other businesses.

CHAPTER 21
APPRECIATE PEOPLE—EVERY DAY

"Our work-a-day lives are filled with opportunities to bless others. The power of a single glance or an encouraging smile must never be underestimated."

G. Richard Rieger

I make an effort to appreciate all the people in my sphere of contact—every day. I praise team members for their achievements, congratulate family, friends and staff on their successes, thank clients for their business, recognize subcontractors and vendors for their contributions, and empathize with those experiencing hardships.

Adopting "an attitude of gratitude" can be the most effective leadership style you embrace. It begins with a focus on the positive qualities of the individuals you come in contact with each day: cheerful, optimistic, thorough, thoughtful, meticulous, friendly, supportive, focused, caring, intelligent, cooperative, dependable, trustworthy, passionate, appreciative. When you "see" these attributes, praise them.

Expressing appreciation to people is almost like creating a testimonial for the people you're recognizing. This is a little unorthodox perhaps, but the end result is language and thoughts that reflect your appreciation for an individual's strengths rather than their faults. When you regularly notice someone's positive attributes, their self-confidence is bolstered and their self-esteem and faith in the company is raised in turn. Team members feel unique, special and competent, and you begin to develop a workforce that is passionate, motivated and successful. How does one appreciate people?

Remember To Say "Thank You"

The two most important words you need to remember are: "thank you"! Everyone who contributes to our success is thanked for his efforts: team members, subcontractors, suppliers and especially clients. If an employee accomplishes a noteworthy feat, I praise them verbally in front of their team. If we receive a glowing testimonial from a customer, I read it at the morning meeting and distribute it to the entire project team, including the office staff who work behind the scenes on every successful job.

One afternoon I received a phone call from a client who wanted me to know what a professional job the mowing team had done at his property.

I met with the mow team the next morning to share the wonderful compliments. When I finished, the whole company applauded, making the mowing crew extremely proud. They have since received numerous compliments from other clients, inspiring them to do an even better job.

Our construction team was working at a project when we decided that three maple trees needed to be removed before the project could continue. I called Fred Burns, a subcontractor who owns Tree Works Unlimited. I explained the situation and asked if he could do the job within three days so our project could continue without significant delays. He told me he would look at his schedule and call me back in the morning. To my surprise, he rearranged his schedule and arrived on our job the next day. Within six hours our construction team was able to continue with its work.

I called Fred to thank him for such quick, professional service. Fred appreciated the compliment and noted that he considered WRE to be one of his best customers. Because of this he always makes our needs a priority. The level of appreciation Fred and I share for each other's company is beneficial to both. To this day we continue to use Fred's tree company as our primary tree-care service firm.

We have used Sylvans Nursery, Inc., located in Westport, Mass. as a major source of our plant material since 1985. Through the years our business has benefited from this relationship and we consistently receive outstanding service from Sylvans' wonderful staff.

During the height of the planting season, Sylvans provides most of our inventory and our weekly purchases are delivered to our site in Woodville. As a rule, their sales manager needs at least two day's notice to pull, organize and load our plant orders before shipping. On one occasion, a client called with a request for several additional plants not on our weekly order. I knew the order was already loaded, but called the sales manager at Sylvans anyway and explained that the additional plants were desperately needed to complete the job, which would allow us to receive final payment (always a strong motivator with us).

Not only did the sales manager locate and load the plants, she offered to deliver the plants right to the job site so we could complete the project on time. The client was happy and gladly made the final payment, and our planting team was grateful that they had all the plants they needed to finish the job that day. I immediately called Sylvans to thank the sales manager, shipping manager and owner for their extraordinary efforts.

I also show my appreciation to our valued clients for their generosity and loyalty to our business. In the past I've sent clients evergreen wreaths right after Thanksgiving each year. The results of these small tokens of appreciation have been amazing. Each client calls or writes a note of thanks for these unexpected gifts.

A gift of thanks doesn't have to be so elaborate. Any symbol of appreciation is greatly appreciated: cards, flowers, a personal thank you or a phone call. A sincere, timely act of appreciation establishes trust, encourages further cooperation and strengthens a relationship that benefits both parties.

When a project is completed, a company receives its financial rewards. An even greater reward, however, is the sense of pride one gets for a job well done and when a client acknowledges the work with a note of thanks. I have received many heartfelt testimonials from satisfied clients through the years. One of these continues to motivate us daily, and I'd like to share it:

Dear Frank:

A heartfelt thanks for transforming our yard into a little piece (or should I say "Peace") of heaven! To say that we LOVE the gardens, paths and fencing is truly an understatement. Words cannot describe their effect or beauty! And the lights - WOW!

We also wanted to commend each and every person involved with the project. Everyone was a pleasure to work with and their professional approach and attention to detail was ever evident. Whether it was Al or Wayne tilling the earth... or Chris and Eric setting the path... Ron's skillful hands crafting a thing of beauty... Rick and Chief lighting the way... and Kathy providing the final glow! All added up to PERFECTION!! We thank you, Frank, for your vision and for providing such a great team of wonderful people to work with.

WRE, Inc....our thanks!!! You have given us a gift we will cherish for years to come!

Thank you - warm regards,
Bill & Maureen Gillick and family

Recognizing individuals for their accomplishments by offering a kind word, extending a handshake or pat on the back, and making a practice of praise has also helped foster a culture in our company that attracts and retains talented, dedicated employees.

Showing gratitude has helped us build a network of dependable, professional subcontractors who are extremely responsive to our clients' needs, and appreciating the efforts of our nursery suppliers has created a reservoir of good will, a commitment to outstanding service and a desire to meet our needs. Fitting testimony that the two most important words you can use everyday are "thank you."

LESSONS LEARNED:

1. The most important thing a business owner can do every day is to show appreciation for staff, clients, subcontractors and vendors.
2. Look for the positive qualities in people and reinforce them with praise.
3. The words "thank you" are a powerful way to acknowledge the value of the people around you.

CHAPTER 23
TRANSFORM YOURSELF

"Be in the present. Learn from the past. Plan for the future"
Spencer Johnson - "The Present"

I had only 15 minutes before my next appointment, and I was feeling a little faint from not eating. I pulled into a McDonald's to grab a cheeseburger, fries and a drink.

My day was not going well. I was late for my first sales appointment, which meant playing catch-up all day long. I was upset that a project hadn't been completed, meaning a delay in the final payment; and the morning meeting with my managers had been tense. (I had received a call from a demanding client who wanted us at her property that day, meaning my crew would have to leave their scheduled job and rush to the client's site, and I lashed out at them when they objected to my change in their plans for the day.)

As I entered the McDonald's parking lot, I felt stressed, frustrated, tense and depressed. I jumped out of my pickup, ordered at the counter, brought the bag of "nutritious" food back to my truck, and gobbled up the burger and fries. After finishing the meal, I looked for my keys so that I could move on to my next appointment. I couldn't find them. I checked my pockets, truck seat and floor. No keys.

Getting more frustrated, I traced my steps back to where I ordered. No keys. I began to get desperate. I checked the truck again. No keys. Thinking they might have fallen into the food bag I threw away in the garbage can, I unceremoniously ripped through the trash looking for them. No luck.

I was close to exploding when something significant happened: I opened my pickup door, sat in my seat and cried for about five minutes. For the next 30 minutes, I talked to myself, analyzing what had happened this day (and many days previously), and came to the realization that I was on the verge of a meltdown. I angered easily and was stressed over the business. I was depressed and easily provoked. I was a devoted "workaholic" who proudly worked 16 hours a day, 6 and one-half days a week. (I relinquished Sunday afternoons for my family.) Seeing all of this for the first time, I came face to face with my own humanity and knew I couldn't continue at the pace I was working. (I never did find my keys. I called the office and had someone bring me a spare set.)

How ironic that losing a set of keys helped me find my life. That defining moment prompted me to seek professionals to help me find my way, discover myself, solve my business, family and personal problems, and help me chart a new course that would be peaceful, happy, healthy, mindful, serene and enlightened.

That very day I called Anna Caruolo, a therapist I had seen briefly in 1997. I told her I desperately needed her counsel to deal with my personal frustrations, business issues and shaky relationships with my wife and three children—quite a plateful! At our first meeting, Anna skillfully prioritized the list so the most pressing issues were dealt with first. With each incremental success, we took on additional issues.

The behavior I exhibited, along with the results of the Burns Depression Inventory and other evaluation sessions, led Anna to believe I was "covertly" depressed. The words hit me hard. Me? Covertly depressed? I had always solved my own problems, I rarely asked for help, and I never seriously considered that my problem could be depression. I was shocked.

However, after reading a book Anna gave me called "I Don't Want to Talk About It," by Terrence Real, I realized that "covert depression" was exactly what I was experiencing: irritability, lack of focus, workaholic behavior, indifference to my wife and family, mood swings, angry outbursts and an overwhelming feeling of sadness with very few moments of happiness. I was able to exist with covert depression but it was no way to live.

Real explains that men with covert depression continue to function, but underlying conditions are largely hidden. This "masked" depression results in burying oneself in work, displaying anger and irritability, and alienating the family. It's estimated that 11 million people in the United States struggle with depression each year, resulting in lost productivity and medical expenses that exceed $47 billion annually. Sadly, this condition goes undiagnosed more often than not; approximately 75 percent of people with depression never get help. This is unfortunate because treatment has a high success rate—as I can happily attest.

Once I came to grips with the diagnosis, Anna and I moved to break down and discuss each issue one by one. She armed me with personal tools and language to use in my interactions with business associates, employees and family members. She helped me develop techniques to reduce my stress, and began to reconstruct me, step by step.

We met twice a month from November 2002 until my last session in August 2004. It was a long, emotional and painful journey at times, and resulted in a sad but amicable divorce from my wife, Penny. I reconnected with my three children, discovered a newfound enthusiasm for the business, learned how to schedule time for my personal life, adopted a healthier attitude and peaceful demeanor, and, in general, began to experience a happy existence.

Beyond therapy, there were other things that helped me make this transformation: frequent exercise, better nutrition and meditation.

Exercise Program

I've always done some exercise but Anna encouraged a scheduled regime. I combine daily jogs with sit-ups, push-ups, frequent walks at the beach, and twice-weekly trips to a health club where I work out with weight machines and the exercise bike. I cool down with some time in the gym shooting basketballs (one of my favorite diversions). The results have been encouraging. I feel healthier, have more energy, handle daily stress better, and take on the day's activities with enthusiasm.

Nutritional Program

For years I have been addicted to sugar in all forms: sugar on my morning cereal, cakes, pies, fudge, candy bars, soda, ice cream. Wow! (I'm tempted as I write this.) A meal wasn't complete unless I had dessert.

Since visiting Pamela Rand, a nutrition and yoga therapist in September 2004, however, my sugar days are over. I now eat more fruits, vegetables and whole-grain foods. I avoid processed foods, high fructose corn syrup and hydrogenated fats. I gave up soda and now drink water, organic juices, and soymilk. My daily diet consists of oatmeal, fruit, soymilk and organic juice in the morning; a protein midday; carbohydrates in the evening with midmorning and afternoon snacks of fruit, yogurt or nuts to help balance blood sugar levels.

On a rare (and special) occasion, I'll treat myself to a dessert, but the candy bars and sugars are gone. To date, I've lost 14 pounds, and rarely experience any of my former sugar-related ups and downs. My goal is to reach 185 pounds, which is 10 pounds more that what I weighed when I graduated from high school 35 years ago! It is amazing how these steps helped eliminate my depression. It was a truly holistic approach to improving my physical, mental and emotional health.

Meditation

Meditation has created additional results that I couldn't have imagined. My meditation practice began after receiving a 50th birthday gift certificate from Lynda Martel for eight weeks of meditation classes at All That Matters, a yoga and wellness center located in Wakefield, R.I.

Lynda had been very supportive through the difficult times I experienced. I was appreciative of the gift but reluctant to sign up. What was meditation like? Would you have to sit cross-legged for hours and chant? In spite of my apprehensions, Lynda assured me it was something I should try.

After attending my first class, I realized how important it was to sit still, find my breath, and be present, mindful and centered. I learned that meditation could be done anywhere: in class, at home, at work or walking at the beach. Now I begin each day with a 10-minute breathing meditation and every Wednesday my meditation instructor, Trish Thornton, holds an hour-long guided meditation class at my house.

Trish taught me various breathing techniques, healing meditations, how to be mindful and in the present, and inspired me to expand my meditation experience. Now, when situations get stressful and I begin to feel frustrated, all it takes is some simple breathing cycles for me to become calm, lower my blood pressure and move forward with confidence.

Meditation may not be for everyone, but it played a major role in changing my behavior and my life. My staff purchased two additional gift certificates so I could continue meditation classes. (They enjoyed the fruits of my peaceful demeanor at work and wanted me to continue that behavior!)

I have since read numerous books on meditation and self-improvement. One I found particularly helpful in understanding "mindful" meditations was *"Wherever You Go There You Are,"* by Jon Kabat-Zinn. Kabat-Zinn advises that by cultivating patience—something that had been in short supply with me—we can cultivate mindfulness and a richer more mature meditation practice results.

"Under the surface of impatience," he writes, "you will find anger, which is the energy of not wanting things to be the way they are, and blaming someone else for it." We need to harness our energies to bring balance to the present moment; with patience lies wisdom. Suspend your judgment. Let each moment be as it is without trying to label it good or bad.

Recently, I drove four members of my company to New England Grows, a horticultural trade show and seminar held in Boston, Mass. each year. The traffic was horrendous. Accidents, delays, detours and inaccurate directions transformed a 90-minute trip into a 3.5-hour nightmare. The drive home was much better, and an hour after leaving Boston we were in Providence enjoying a nice dinner. At the dinner table, each of my managers remarked how calm and serene I remained throughout our morning drive in spite of the stress; even when we entered a tunnel by mistake, got lost in the center of Boston, and fought our way through tremendous construction traffic and detours. They asked how I did it.

I replied that I have learned to accept the conditions in the present moment. That day's conditions included the traffic, accidents and detours—a fact of life. I couldn't change the situation, but by accepting the moments as they unfolded, I was able to remain calm and use the situation to engage in meaningful conversation with each person in the car with me.

In his book *"Failing Forward,"* John C. Maxwell says, "A problem is something that can be solved. A fact of life is something that must be accepted." We waste so much time and energy worrying about potential problems that may occur today, tomorrow or the next day. The truth is, we have no control over what is yet to come. It's a fact of life we must accept regardless of the outcome. Why worry about it? Especially days in advance! My new strategy is to stay in the present, use the lessons I've learned in the past to deal with what is happening now, and formulate plans for the future.

It is a liberating feeling being in the present moment; listening attentively to someone speaking to you; observing a glorious sunrise or sunset; enjoying the sounds of a gurgling stream; watching hawks fly; breathing in fresh air; and working on a project with your full attention. By being open and attentive we grow and learn, developing the fullness of our being. Once the fullness of our being is experienced, we can share our enthusiasm, vitality, spirit and openness with others.

Meditation is not just a part of my life; it is my life. Whether in the shower, jogging, driving, walking, attending meetings or having lunch, the lessons learned from meditation—being mindful, peaceful, focused and in the present moment—are felt.

Creating Space For Practice

To enhance my meditation practice, I designed and built a meditation garden outside my home. Previously, this small, private backyard featured a tiny patch of lawn, a farm stone wall and a large concrete slab that served as a patio area. Viewing this space from my living room, I envisioned a wonderful setting for a meditation garden. I soon transformed my backyard into an Oriental landscape featuring a water fall, dry stone stream bed, landscape lighting and outdoor music. A beautiful wooden deck now covers the unsightly concrete slab and provides the perfect spot for three Adirondack chairs and an outdoor fire pit. The river-rock stream winds its way through several stunning garden beds and alongside field stone steps planted with low sedum and thyme between them. The garden beds are filled with varieties of shrubs, perennials and specimen plants selected to enhance the Oriental look of the landscape. An occasional planter overflowing with annuals provides color and interest all season long.

This peaceful, tranquil space is the perfect area to relax, read and reflect. A dream come true, thanks to my two sons, Frank and Jason, who helped install the plantings and outdoor sound system with employees Greg Belanger and Cathy Caddick. Our talented masons, Ryan Gardiner and Arthur Gardner, transformed the farm wall into a beautiful backdrop for

their stunning water feature. Our carpenter, Ron Liese, built the custom-designed deck, and our talented lighting designer, Kathy Quinn, installed fixtures that illuminate the area with a warm, subtle glow.

From April to December, the garden is a place for meals, weekly meditation classes, parties, and frequent hours of reflective reading. A quiet relaxing space like this is

Frank's meditation garden with Oriental plantings, wooden deck, waterfalls, landscape lighting and flat-stone path.

priceless. As the pace of our daily lives continues to increase, it is important—no, imperative—that we create a place to relax and reflect, whether it is in our backyard, a local park, or in our own mind.

I supplement my meditation practice with reading. Don Miquel Ruiz's book, "The Four Agreements," has inspired me to incorporate these agreements into my daily life. They are a constant reminder and guide. I strive to embody the agreements. I believe personal freedom and true happiness will be my reward as I transform into the master of my own life.

The Four Agreements Are:

1. **Be impeccable with your word.** Always speak with integrity. Say only what you mean. Use the power of your word toward truth and love.

2. Don't take anything personally. Nothing others do is because of you. What others say is a projection of their own reality. Be immune to the opinions and actions of others.

3. Don't make assumptions. Find the courage to ask questions and express what you really want. Communicate with others clearly so to avoid misunderstandings, sadness and drama.

4. Always do your best. Your best is going to change from moment to moment, when you are healthy or sick. Under any circumstance, do your best, and you will avoid self-judgment, self-abuse and regret.

These are powerful, simple concepts, but not so easy to put into practice. Before understanding the power of these agreements, I would take any criticism personally and feel discouraged all day. Today I acknowledge criticism as an opportunity for improvement, not a personal attack.

I used to make frequent pessimistic comments to staff members without realizing the impact my words had on their motivation and enthusiasm. Today I choose my words carefully, try to be clear and express myself with words of optimism and encouragement. In her song, *"If I Could Turn Back Time,"* Cher sings, "Words, like weapons, wound some time." I am much more aware of my words today, especially since, as the owner, the impact of what I say can have a lasting effect (good and bad) on staff morale.

The one agreement that continues to elude me (and some of my employees) is to not make assumptions. Making false assumptions (and not communicating clearly) causes most of our daily problems in the business, and most of my personal problems with others. Although not an easy habit to overcome, this agreement can be conformed to with awareness and practice.

Even with all its challenges, I now find life enjoyable, precious, rewarding, exciting and fun. Every day I wake up energized and thankful, ready to embrace each and every moment. I try to maintain an evenness of emotions because I know that "successes aren't forever and failures aren't fatal." I have discarded the notion that I'll be happy and successful when I pay off all my debts, when I make a greater profit, or when I'm a well-known speaker because I realize now that every moment of each day I am successful, I am happy, and I am fulfilled.

With all the successes, defeats, tragedies and accomplishments in my life, it has been, and will be, the perfect journey!

LESSONS LEARNED:

1. Solicit professional help to deal with serious problems you are not able or qualified to handle.
2. Regular exercise and a sound nutrition program play a key role in reducing stress, increasing energy and creating a healthier "you."
3. Meditation is a great stress-reducing tool and will help you feel serene and calm.
4. Be in the present. Enjoy each moment as it evolves. Learn from the past. Plan for a wonderful journey.

CHAPTER 24
NEVER GIVE UP!

"Never give up. Never give in. Never, never, never. In nothing great or small, large or petty, never give in except to conviction of honor and good sense."
Sir Winston Churchill
- Speech at Harrow, October 29, 1941

These inspirational words by Winston Churchill have great relevancy to me this winter of 2005. January 24 marked the 40th anniversary of Churchill's death and the opening of the Churchill Museum at the Cabinet War Rooms in London, England. The museum is the first in Great Britain dedicated to the life, achievements and legacy of the greatest Briton ever: Sir Winston Churchill.

I visited the Cabinet War Rooms in May 2004 and was overwhelmed with the operations, leadership efforts and human sacrifice required to direct the war efforts and to make momentous decisions under bleak conditions. It's hard to comprehend what the British went through during the bombing of London. The personal sacrifices made to defeat Nazism and preserve freedom were staggering.

Churchill's "finest hour" may have been as prime minister from May 1940 to July 1945, but, equally important, and as inspirational, was his heroic, sometimes lonely, stand against the Nazis and the rise of expansionist Germany in the decade before WWII.

Against both public and government opinion, Churchill persisted in his public stance of advocating increased military preparedness to stop Hitler. His vision proved prophetic when he became prime minister in 1940 and he displayed the exact leadership qualities needed to help win WWII.

I have been a student and admirer of Churchill for years. I feel we can all learn from his courage, leadership skills and writings, all of which continue to inspire 60 years after the end of the Second World War. At the beginning of World War II, Churchill proclaimed, "we shall not fail." His words became a motto to me as I faced my own adversities through the years.

In his book *"Failing Forward,"* John C. Maxwell, says: "To achieve your dreams, you must embrace adversity and make failure a regular part of your life. If you're not failing, you're probably not really moving forward."

I've experienced several adversities since 1989: a cash-flow crisis that almost destroyed my business; fire that destroyed my property; being struck by lighting; loss of revenue from drought, water bans and severe winter weather; depression; divorce. These adversities helped shape my business, my philosophy and my personal life.

Cash-flow Crisis

This book wouldn't have been written if I listened to my banker in 1992 when he suggested filing for bankruptcy, but the thought of admitting failure and living with the stigma of bankruptcy was not an option for me.

The road to financial recovery was long, difficult and extremely painful for my wife, three children and me. The sacrifices they endured to ensure our survival were selfless and incredible. With only enough money for bare necessities, our lives were basically just an existence for several years. I'll never be able to thank them enough for their commitment, nor would I ever put them through another situation like that again.

To prevent this type of economic suicide from ever repeating, I first constructed a business plan in 1992 and continue to revise it regularly renewing my dedication to use it as my guide when making business decisions. A cash-flow crisis like the one I experienced in 1992 will never be repeated.

Struck By Lightning

On July 14, 1989 I experienced one of nature's most powerful forces when I received an indirect hit by lightning. I recovered completely thanks to the rapid response of a rescue squad, and the doctors and nurses at Kent County Hospital in Warwick, R.I.

That afternoon I was working on a landscape project in East Greenwich, R.I. when thunderstorms suddenly appeared. At the first sign of rain, the planting designer and I ran for cover to the customer's porch while three workers jumped into my pickup. After a downpour, the storm abated, the sun came out, and we began to arrange trees and shrubs in the front yard amongst several 60- to 70-foot oak trees.

Soon, the rain, thunder and lightning reappeared, and several brilliant bolts of lightning lit up the sky as the storm moved closer. We again retreated to the porch, discussed plant placement, the weather, and safe places to be in a thunderstorm. I was sitting against a brick wall and part of the front metal door and doorbell. Suddenly, there was a huge flash, a loud snap and a crash in the front yard. I felt a surge of electricity in my lower back and cried out in pain as I slumped to the porch floor, semiconscious.

A fire department member later told me that a bolt of lighting struck the telephone box near a large oak tree, blowing the bark off the tree

30 feet up its trunk. The current then traveled into the house through the telephone wires (melting them) and exited the front doorbell. I was wet, leaning on a metal door near the doorbell, and a very good conductor for the current.

(I pieced together the rest of the events from eyewitness accounts, medical reports and the rescue squad, as I do not remember the hour and a half after being struck.)

In the ambulance I had no feeling in my arms, hands or feet. During the short trip to the hospital, I went into respiratory arrest, which was quickly corrected by the rescue squad. Once in the emergency room, I was still only semiconscious and it would be 45 minutes before I had complete feeling again.

Fully conscious, I began a three-day odyssey in the ICU and ECCU units, undergoing a battery of blood tests, x-rays and examinations by numerous specialists including a neurologist, cardiologist, pulmonary and respiratory specialists, bone specialist, and a general practitioner to determine if there was permanent organ damage. Fortunately, the results of all tests proved negative. They did show that I have a strong heart and because I was healthy, I recovered completely with no lasting damage.

God looked after me during this episode and I learned several valuable lessons from this "enlightening" experience:

• Lightning is deadly and life too precious not to take extreme precautions to protect yourself (and others) from the effects of electrical storms.
• Stay clear of trees, bodies of water, telephones, metal doors, doorbells and other electrical outlets during a storm.
• Do not take unnecessary chances with workers, friends, and a homeowner's personal safety when on a job site during a storm.
• A safe place to be during electrical storms is in a vehicle with rubber tires—not outside trying to complete a project in the rain!
• Safety MUST be a constant priority since lightning is unpredictable and deadly, and should never be challenged.

I was lucky to survive and be surrounded by loving, caring family members, friends, customers, hospital staff and rescue personnel who helped me through this traumatic experience.

Fire!

I remember vividly the February night a panic-stricken tenant called screaming that our Christmas shop was on fire. I jumped out of bed and peered out the window to see flames reaching 25 feet in the air from the north end of the two-story pine board retail shop on our property.

I immediately called the Hope Valley Fire Department and encouraged them to get to us fast, since our 1761 rental house was only 20 feet away from the burning shop. I quickly donned my clothes and rushed to the burning building. Snow and sleet made the trip for the fire trucks extremely dangerous but within just eight minutes the first truck arrived, driven by my brother-in-law, Ray Bader.

Thanks to the efforts of the firemen the 1761 house was saved. Unfortunately, the two-story retail shop was completely gutted and our shop inventory, including an extensive collection of irreplaceable German nutcrackers was destroyed. (One of the handmade nutcrackers stood six feet tall and was one of only 60 in the world.)

Watching the fire rip through the roof and second floor, I felt total despair and a terrible sadness. My brother Doug, father Frank Jr., father-in-law Ray Bader, and I had built this two-story Christmas Shop in 1986. Remembering the effort we all put into its construction I became emotional, but soon the reality of what was happening struck me and I quickly checked with my tenants to make sure they were OK. I also walked around to thank the firemen who had done a fantastic job under extremely hazardous conditions.

The following day, after the flames had died out but with the structure still smoldering, I realized how fortunate it was that no one was seriously hurt in the fire. (I found out later that my brother-in-law suffered a serious back injury that night.) Thanks to Ray's quick arrival, the 1761 house was saved and no other injuries occurred.

Almost immediately many neighbors, friends and employees called to offer assistance. I was overwhelmed with generous offers to store items, help rebuild the shop, or provide anything else we needed. It was a tremendous, heartfelt outpouring of giving that I will never forget.

Once the insurance agents, fire marshals and other professionals completed their work—an electrical short caused the fire, possibly due to a squirrel chewing on electrical wires in the storage building located next to the shop—I began to formulate a plan to rebuild.

I firmly believe there is a silver lining to every dark cloud. This tragedy gave us the opportunity to build a new structure that could better serve our growing company. We created office space for our designers, a spacious conference room for employee and client meetings, much-needed storage space, and a showroom for sales presentations and horticultural lectures. The two-story building was rebuilt over the next eight months with new offices, air-conditioning and heating, plumbing, and an up-to-date fire detector and alarm system.

I always had a vision of creating a design showcase featuring our many landscaping services on the property. Within a week of describing my vision, designer Jenn Judge drew up a plan that incorporated all these features into the landscape.

Over the next two years, the new WRE Landscape Design Showcase was completed. This impressive two-acre display features themed gardens and a variety of design elements for our customers to consider for their own landscapes: paver patios and walkways, stone walls, fish ponds, waterfalls, wooden pergolas, a bridge, arbors, gazebo, landscape lighting, irrigation, and underground cisterns to capture and recycle rain runoff.

The showcase was dedicated in the summer of 2003. The WRE Landscape Design Showcase is the only one of its kind in southern New England. It could not have happened without a tremendous effort from the WRE staff (who donated many volunteer hours), and substantial contributions from local suppliers.

Author John C. Maxwell also says: "Every major difficulty you face in life is a fork in the road. You choose which track you will head down, toward breakdown or breakthrough." I chose breakthrough.

Revenue Shortfalls

Being in a weather-dependent business we have experienced numerous natural disasters: hurricanes, floods and winter wind damage. None, however, have affected our landscape business as much as periodic summer droughts and the resulting water bans. Two out of the last four summers have been dry enough to prompt communitywide water restrictions in almost every market area we serve.

Water bans create a domino effect on our industry. They prohibit planting, reduce lawn mowing and maintenance, jeopardize the health of trees, shrubs and perennials covered under our money-back warranty, and discourage clients from spending money on landscaping. The effect on horticultural businesses in terms of reduced sales, lost revenue, layoffs, warranty replacements and financial setbacks can be fatal.

In my early years, I would go into a panic anticipating droughts and their detrimental effect on our landscape business. Not any more. Before the season even begins, I educate my staff about steps we can take to minimize the effect of a sustained drought and water bans on our clients' landscapes.

Drought is not a new problem, nor is it one that will go away. Water restrictions and bans are conditions that will impact our business for the foreseeable future. My proactive, multiphase action plans for dealing with annual summer water restrictions typifies the approach needed to be implemented by everyone—droughts are a fact of life.

We can address the problems of how to maintain our clients' plants during restrictions, how to complete projects in the summer, how to prepare a landscape for drought, how to use drought-tolerant plants, and how to conserve and recycle water. I have devised an educational program to prepare my staff, our clients, suppliers and the public on water conservation in the landscape as well as in a home. Through workshops, seminars, pamphlets, direct-mail newsletters and personal meetings, the conservation message is getting out.

The main process I discuss is xeriscaping, which entails water conservation in the landscape, effective mulching, the use of compost in planting and top dressing, soil amendments like hydro gels, mowing lawns higher and leaving the grass clippings, watering infrequently but deeply in the morning, use of drip irrigation, collecting water run-off into rain barrels and cisterns, checking all faucets, nozzles and connections, choosing drought-tolerant plants, and grouping plants with similar water needs together. Following these suggestions improves the survival rate of landscape plantings, allows landscaping projects to continue through the summer, and encourages clients to think about and practice water conservation all year long.

To help our clients maintain the health of plants already installed, we purchased a fire truck with a 1,000-gallon tank, which can be used for supplementary watering until nature assists.

Overcoming Personal Adversity

An important lesson I learned in the process of dealing with overwhelming personal or business problems is to seek out professional assistance to help understand and overcome those problems.

When the symptoms of my depression crippled my ability to function effectively, I called Anna to undertake a therapy program. When I realized that my eating habits were affecting my health, energy and motivation level, I contacted Pam to construct a nutrition program. With a recommendation from Lynda, I enrolled in a meditation class that continues today under the expert guidance of Trish.

When my employees requested tools to enhance their team-building and communication skills, I brought in a business coach, Bob Cohen, to run communication and team building workshops. During the early stages of developing our current budget program, I hired a consultant to devise an Excel program that would measure vehicle, equipment and personnel costs.

As accounting is not one of my strong suits, I later hired a professional, Terry Malaghan, to do the job and to serve as an advisor that would help us grow and become more professional. To integrate computer technology and software into our daily operations, I hired Ken as our systems manager, who helped us change the way we do business for greater efficiency and productivity. In 1998, I hired Lynda to become our vice president to create processes for our business as we grew from 12 employees to 35 employees.

My personal growth, advancements and success are in great measure due to the talented, helpful, and professional people I work with. Not only are they skilled experts, but they are also my friends. The relationships I have been able to forge are priceless. As a result of my growth and achievements, I can extend their professional abilities to my staff, family and friends. Seeking help from professionals to help you tackle significant problems is not a sign of weakness; it is an indication of wisdom.

Never give up!

LESSONS LEARNED:

1. Take inspiration from those who have overcome personal adversities and tragedies, and who maintained their beliefs in spite of opposing views.
2. Always look for the silver lining in the dark clouds and you will find it.
3. Respond to problems with an energetic and pro-active approach.
4. Regardless of the obstacles between you and your goals, never give up!

CHAPTER 25
THOSE WHO INSPIRED

"I owe my accomplishments, passions, and successes to those who witting-ly or unwittingly inspired me. Thank you!"

Frank Crandall

I clearly remember what my Grade 8 math teacher at Central Junior High School in Bedford, Texas wrote in my yearbook at the end of the school year: "Learn from everyone you meet. Take their best qualities, incorporate them, grow to be a better person, and someday you'll be president." Although he never specifically indicated president of what, I am happy to be president of my own company today.

I took his advice to heart and over the next 40 years I tried to emulate the positive qualities I found in friends, family, colleagues, business owners, teachers, coaches, and current and historical national figures. I believe I have become a better person as a result of their inspiring words and deeds.

Frank And Betty Crandall: My Parents

My mom and dad were huge inspirations to my brother, Doug, sister, Lorie, and me. Their principles of "hard work" definitely transferred to all three children. Dad worked two jobs most of the time: mornings on his father's potato farm and second shift at Harris Intertype, a printing press firm.

My experiences growing up on a farm remain with me: working long hours in the fields, battling nature's vagaries, dealing with insect and disease problems, learning to live with minimal financial return.

One characteristic my father always displayed, especially with complex tasks, was patience. He would take apart an old tractor, carefully disassemble, categorize and restore all parts to mint condition (or fabricate a new part if the old one was beyond repair), re-paint the engine and the body, and eventually restore the tractor to its original condition. This process often took months. I was always amazed at my father's skill and patience with this type of tedious activity. I strive to incorporate this characteristic into my own repertoire of personal qualities. Mom was always there supporting our needs, taking us to practices after school, encouraging our efforts and praising our accomplishments. She always fostered a philosophy of tolerance and equality.

Both parents encouraged personal independence, participation in sports, work on weekends, and making purchases only when we earned enough money of our own.

I started my own landscape business when I was a junior in high school. Dad suggested I buy an older pickup to haul materials to my customers but still keep expenses down. They let me use their property to raise trees, store mulch, and occasionally dad let me use his 1952 Ford bucket tractor, which was handy on bigger jobs.

Most important, my parents were my compasses. They gave me advice and direction when it was needed, supported me during tough times and applauded my every success.

Mom and dad, happily married for 54 years, are a loving, resilient model of stability in a turbulent world.

Dr. Dorothy Crandall Bliss: Aunt Dot

My Aunt Dot was first in inspiring my interest in plants, teaching, photography and giving presentations.

Dorothy grew up on the Crandall Farm, graduated from Rhode Island State College with bachelor's and master's degrees, and earned her doctorate at the University of Tennessee. In 1949 she became a biology professor at Randolph Macon Women's College in Lynchburg, Va. where she taught until retiring in 1983.

I was always thrilled when Aunt Dot presented her famous slide shows, which featured many dramatic close-ups of colorful flowers she photographed at parks all over the world. My love for botany began with those early slide shows and nature walks around the farm with Aunt Dot. At an early age, I began to learn the Latin names for plants so that I could have conversations with my aunt about them. In later years, I took my own photographs and created slide shows which I consider a wonderful combination of education and visual art.

Again, following in Aunt Dot's footsteps, I attended URI, majored in botany and education, and eventually become a high school biology teacher. Many of the skills I learned from my aunt were put to use in my classroom.

I still visit Dorothy at her Lynchburg home to talk about plants—using as many Latin names as I can remember—assist with her landscape maintenance, and visit the Randolph Macon Botanic Garden established by her in 1994 as a legacy of her love of plants and teaching.

At 89, Aunt Dot is still going strong—in spite of a recent hip replacement—giving lectures and leading botanical garden nature walks. Aunt Dot's inspiration motivated both my educational and horticultural careers, but her most valuable lesson stems from her appreciation of ecology and the environment, something we need to instill in others in order to protect and preserve what we have.

And last, but not least, if it wasn't for Aunt Dot's financial generosity in the early 1990s to help us pay overdue debts, WRE would have ceased to exist. I will be eternally grateful for her faith in me.

Sal Augeri: Coach And Teacher

In 1967, when I moved from Texas to attend Westerly High School, Sal Augeri was my football coach. As an incoming sophomore, I continued my football career as an aspiring quarterback. I started the first three games of the season, but Sal replaced me with a more experienced senior for the balance of the year so that I could learn more about the position.

Sal was an inspiration to all the players, and always encouraged us to do our best. He demanded superior effort, even in practices. He firmly believed that the sacrifices we made at double sessions before a season started, and at grueling practices during the season, would pay off in the end. Westerly's (R.I.) football reputation was renowned. Teamwork was the benchmark of our football team, with everyone working together as a unit. Tradition played an important role in motivating players.

The most important lesson I learned was to set goals and strive for excellence. Sal's football teams exuded excellence and his teams ultimately won two R.I. Super Bowl Championships—his overall coaching record was 78 wins, 27 losses and four ties—and Sal was voted into the R.I. Coaches Hall of Fame. The Westerly High School athletic field is named in his honor.

I'm glad I was a member of the football program with Sal as coach. Although we didn't win a championship during my time with the team, Sal taught me many lessons that continue to benefit me today.

Ray Bader: My Father-in-law

I first met Ray, or Mr. Bader as I addressed him for years, in 1969 after bringing Penny home from one of our first dates. He was wearing an Electric Boat (now the Electric Boat Division of General Dynamics) security guard's uniform. I learned that was only one of many jobs Ray did well. Ray left school in the eighth grade to support his mother, but by the time I met him, he was an expert carpenter, electrician, plumber, landlord and farmer. All self-taught! Ray was the most giving, helpful person I've ever met, always doing what he could to help people, especially newly married families.

Ray became an integral part of WRE's development. He assisted in the building of our Christmas Shop and our wreath-making shack, he waited on customers (he loved to talk with people) and he was our driver for the Christmas hayrides. I was inspired to become more like Ray: helpful, giving, friendly.

The most remarkable thing I witnessed Ray do occurred in our Masonic lodge when he gave a 45-minute lecture about the history of the Master Masons without notes and never missing a word. I was impressed and overwhelmed at that feat.

Ray died in 1993 at the age of 73. At his church service, I eulogized a truly great, self-made man; a man who was devoted to his wife and family, dedicated to helping others, and open to learning as many skills as possible on his own. Ray's life is an inspiration to me, and the memory of his friendly, generous spirit lives on.

Neil Van Sloun: Founder, Sylvans Nursery, Inc.

Neil Van Sloun is one of the truly great businessmen in the New England horticultural industry. Neil is the founder of Sylvans Nursery in Westport, Mass. His company supplies New England—and other regions—with landscape nursery stock. Sylvans is well known for its excellent selection of landscape plants, helpful and professional staff, and superb customer service. Many times I have to make last-minute requests to meet a client's need and Sylvans comes through each time.

When my business grew to the point of needing an employee manual, Neil sent his company's handbook as a reference. When I wanted to create a product catalog with plant codes and retail pricing, Neil provided us with a CD of Sylvans' inventory, code numbers, and wholesale pricing which we were able to download into our computer system to create our own inventory database of plants, codes and retail pricing. Neil's generosity has helped make our company more professional and successful.

During the early 1990s, when our company was experiencing critical cash flow problems, Neil stood by me even though we owed his company nearly $20,000. He made special arrangements for me, and I was able to pay something on our balance each time I purchased and paid for a new shipment of plants. This benevolent act helped WRE survive. Two years later, I had paid off my debt. To this day I hold a great sense of loyalty to Neil and sincerely appreciate his faith in me.

Even beyond his generous nature, Neil has an optimistic philosophy and a calm, friendly personality; traits that I try to emulate myself. Neil is most remarkable for his boundless optimism. I once asked him how a summer's drought was affecting his sales. He admitted that sales were off a little but pointed out that disease problems were way down and that his crews now had time to clean up the yard and the stock so that they would have better plants to sell to their customers when the rain returned.

I have never heard Neil utter a negative word. I often compare him to Dr. Pangloss in Voltaire's novel *"Candide."* Candide experiences disaster after disaster but Dr. Pangloss remarks, "It's still the best of all possible worlds."

Neil is the epitome of an honest, hard-working, innovative businessman who lives in full integrity—a style that horticultural business owners like me can, and should, emulate.

John Tickner: Owner, Babcock & Helliwell Insurance

I started using John's insurance company in 1987 for vehicle and business liability insurance, homeowner insurance and workmen's compensation coverage.

During our financial crisis of 1991-1992, I was faced with a severe cash flow crunch—I couldn't pay my insurance bill for the coming year—and, if I didn't renew my insurance coverage, I would have to close up the business. John met with me and I explained my situation. Without hesitation he said Babcock & Helliwell would pay for my insurance, and I could pay them back when it was possible for me to do so. I couldn't believe it! Because of John's generosity and faith in me, WRE was able to stay open for business. It took me two years but I paid off that bill and have stayed loyal to John's company ever since. The level of service John provides is always top-notch; he is always there to help whenever we have a claim.

In February of 2001, when our Christmas Shop burned down, John was there the next day with appropriate company representatives. Checks were forthcoming within three weeks, and the building was rebuilt by early summer as a result.

Over the years John and I have become good friends and now he and his wife, Carroll, are my landlords. I will never forget what John did for WRE. To this day, I continue to run my business with integrity, generosity and professionalism as my guiding principles; principles that John has always exhibited toward me.

Ken Mazur: WRE Systems Manager

Until I met Ken Mazur from the Computer Lab in 1993, I was a neophyte when it came to computers. When WRE's only computer died, Ken led us through the maze (pun intended) of computer hardware and software products. Little did I know that my first purchase of a Quadra 605 Macintosh computer would begin an 12-year journey of gradual changes, upgrades and expansions to our computer systems.

Today there isn't a facet of our business that doesn't benefit from Ken's recommendations. He not only introduced me to the wonders of computer technology, he changed the way we did business as a result of using the computers to analyze raw data and turn them into useful information.

We now use computers to produce estimates, do monthly billing, create PowerPoint presentations and develop marketing materials. Ken showed us how to view our daily processes differently and he designed programs and installed systems to meet our changing needs. The increased efficiency and productivity have been amazing. We are a much more successful company thanks to Ken. With extreme patience and guidance, Ken and my staff have helped bring me into the computer age.

Ken is more to me than a systems manager; he has become a friend and confidante. His kind words, humorous comments, constant encouragement and years of dedication have helped me through business growth and problems, and my difficult personal times.

Lynda Martel: Business Consultant

Lynda arrived at WRE in 1998 at a critical time in the company's development. With a corporate background and years of experience in advertising and marketing, she was the right person to help our business become more professional and bring us to a higher level within the horticultural field.

As our VP, Lynda helped develop a five-year business plan, strengthen our distinctive brand, and, with Ken, helped refine our plant inventory and pricing program. She also managed all our marketing, advertising and customer communications programs, and helped create the GEM Business Seminars, which we operated from 2001 to 2003.

As our human resources manager, Lynda updated our employee handbook and created job descriptions for each position along with corresponding pay scales and benefit levels. She helped me delegate responsibilities, empower our managers and team leaders, and put into place valuable policies for peaceful conflict resolution. Her efforts in making WRE a stronger, more organized and successful company were truly staggering.

Although her business skills were always evident as our company grew, it was Lynda's personal advice to me, as a friend, that helped me let go of the frustration, anger and lack of focus I had been experiencing. She put me on a different path. Lynda helped me learn to be in the present, deal with problems head on, listen to criticisms objectively, become more focused, remain calm in the midst of chaos, and grow on a professional level.

Anna Caruolo: Clinical Social Worker

I first met Anna in the late 1980s at Grasslands Turf Farm in Kingston, R.I. She and her husband, Bob, owned a sod farm at that time. It was their courteous service and helpful education on the proper installation and care for sod that helped my crew and me learn how to install sod lawns correctly and successfully for our clients. I never forgot their generous help.

When I needed to see a counselor in the late 1990s, Anna was recommended. She had retired from the turf business and had started a career as a therapist. Although my visits with Anna in 1997 were brief, I felt comfortable with her caring, supportive, professional style. So, when I needed a professional therapist in 2003, I called Anna again.

This was a traumatic time for my wife, my children, family, employees, friends and me. Anna helped me overcome "covert depression," handle several overwhelming employee issues, re-connect with my children, deal with my divorce, and regain control of my life. As a result, I'm happy, focused, confident and positive.

Anna also helped me discover the important balance between work, family and my own life. She gave me tools to relieve stress, exercises to build stamina, nutritional guidance to improve my overall health, and breathing exercises and meditation techniques to help me relax. I learned how to deal with difficult situations as they came up, use appropriate words to communicate my feelings and take proper actions when needed, resulting in a "win/win" situation for all involved.

Anna has inspired me to enjoy the present, learn from past mistakes, plan for an exciting future and have fun.

Roger Staubach: Football Quarterback

My first memory of Roger Staubach was as the Heisman Award-winning quarterback that led his Alma Mater, Navy, to a 9-1 regular season record and a number two national ranking in 1963. In 1964 Roger was drafted by the Dallas Cowboys, but didn't play professional football with the team until 1969 due to his Naval commitment.

Living in Texas at the time, I instantly became a huge Cowboys and Roger Staubach fan. He was an inspiration to many high school football players, and I was no exception. My quarterback number in high school was "12," the same as Roger's. Today's sports "heroes" are lacking the fine qualities that Roger Staubach had during his football career, and in his business and charitable endeavors after retirement.

While I never matched Roger's athletic skills on the field, he provided me with many lessons to live by off the field: integrity, charity, responsibility and a competitive nature. Roger was once quoted as saying: "Spectacular achievements come from unspectacular preparation," and, "Confidence doesn't come out of nowhere. It's a result of something ... hours and days and weeks and years of constant work and dedication."

Wise words we need to remember.

John Muir: Environmentalist

I first became aware of environmentalist John Muir in the mid-1970s when I presented a 30-minute film that profiled his life and adventures in Yosemite to my tenth grade biology class.

Muir was a great champion of the environment and a colorful writer. No one was more instrumental in protecting Yosemite under the United States' national park program. Even presidents sought his counsel. In 1903, President Theodore Roosevelt and Muir had long talks about conservation while camping together at Glacier Point in Yosemite. Away from reporters and civilization, these two great men spent three days together camping, hiking and exploring the splendor of Yosemite. As a result, President Roosevelt entered Yosemite into the national park system.

Roosevelt galvanized progressive conservation and Muir galvanized the preservation movement. Their meeting of the minds symbolized the environmental leadership the 21st century would increasingly ask of the National Park Service.

Muir served as the first president and one of the founders of the Sierra Club, played a prominent role in the creation of several national parks, and wrote hundreds of newspaper and magazine articles and several books expounding on the virtues of conservation and the natural world. His journals serve as a stirring reminder of how precious our national treasures are. His written descriptions of the mountains, lakes, trees, plant life and animal life of the area are a "must read."

Muir once noted, "Everybody needs beauty as well as bread—places to play in and pray in, where nature may heal and give strength to body and soul." In today's fast-paced, high-tech world, Muir's words are even more compelling. His environmental views helped preserve thousands of acres of national landscapes and his foresight and passion were critical in saving spectacular resources for future generations to enjoy.

As a writer, Muir taught the people of his time (and ours) the importance of experiencing and protecting our natural heritage. His written observations contributed greatly to the creation of Yosemite, Sequoia, Mount Rainier, the Petrified Forest and Grand Canyon National parks, a legacy of treasures we can all enjoy.

"The battle we have fought, and are still fighting for the forests is a part of the eternal conflict between right and wrong, and we cannot expect to see the end of it. ... So we must count on watching and striving for these trees, and should always be glad to find anything so surely good and noble to strive for," Muir once said.

As a horticulturalist, I couldn't agree more. John Muir's life and passion for the environment have been an inspiration to me since I first learned about this most amazing man.

Winston Churchill: Prime Minister

No other public figure in the 20th century inspired so many people during WWII and his voluminous books and marvelous quotes continue to inspire today. I have found Churchill to be an intriguing individual to study.

Churchill entered Parliament in 1901 at the age of 26. In 1904 he left the Conservative Party to join the Liberals (in part out of calculation because the Liberals were the coming party), and in its ranks he soon achieved high office. He became home secretary in 1910 and first lord of the admiralty in 1911. Thus it was as political head of the Royal Navy at the outbreak of the First World War in 1914 that he stepped onto the world stage.

In 1935 Churchill warned the House of Commons of the importance of "self-preservation ... against the ever advancing sources of authority and despotism," and promoted his views on building up the British forces and to stop Hitler's expansionist policies.

Despite much political criticism and public hostility, Churchill stood by his views, which proved prophetic. When the moment of final confrontation between Britain and Hitler came in 1940, he stood out as the one man in whom the nation could place its trust. He had decried the prewar appeasement policies of the Conservative leaders Baldwin and Chamberlain.

When Chamberlain lost the confidence of Parliament, Churchill was installed in the premiership and he led the free world in the defeat of the Nazis.

Churchill exhibited tremendous strength of character during extremely difficult conditions. His quotes motivated, instilled pride, and inspired a country and a free world, although he humbly denied this fact during a 1954 address to Parliament: "I have never accepted what many people have kindly said—namely that I inspired the nation. Their will was resolute and remorseless, and as it proved, unconquerable. It fell to me to express it."

Churchill displayed outstanding leadership skills during WWII. His talents for public speaking and writing generated many speeches that were broadcast to his countrymen and the world, galvanizing them to defeat the Nazis and Imperial Japan.

I have used many of Churchill's quotes in this book. The previous chapter features one that makes a very important point: never, ever, give up. Regardless of the unpopularity of your opinions or views, if they are based in integrity, honor and goodwill, follow your instincts and persevere for eventually you will succeed.

There have been many more individuals that have influenced my development, but these individuals hold a special place in my heart. Most of my personal qualities can be traced back to the inspirational people who wittingly (or otherwise) helped shape them.

As I move forward on my path to personal improvement, growth and success, I will no doubt meet new friends, business people and horticulturalists from whom I will continue to learn.

CHAPTER 26
THE JOURNEY NEVER ENDS

And so I return to my place in the garden; still on the path of learning and evolving. I may have completed this book but I feel my journey has just begun. Everything in my life continues to evolve as I learn more, do more, and expand as a human being. My business also continues to evolve and I fully expect it to transform over time.

I will negotiate my way through each new transformation with greater confidence and ease thanks to the wisdom gained from important lessons I learned in the past—lessons that will serve as a guide on my journey in the future. I'd like to share these core insights so you can benefit from them as you venture along on your own life's journey.

Maintain Balance

Physics proves that things in this universe eventually expire when out of balance with other forces in its surroundings. Remember that your work is only one part of life's equation. Your professional career should be a means to an end, not the "end-all, be-all" of your life. Create a balance between work and family, scheduling time for both. I learned this lesson the hard way, and the price I paid was my 32-year marriage, and a close relationship with my children. Since reducing the amount of time I spend at work I have reconnected with my three children and my grandson, spending as much time with them as I possibly can.

My failed marriage to Penny has been the hardest lesson. Looking back on the twists and turns of our winding path together, it is hard to know even now what could or should have been done to change the outcome. But, here we are. We made our decisions based on knowledge we had at the time—and there is no revising what has been done. But, by remaining true to my own self, by being honest and sincere, by being compassionate and considerate and holding her in a place most dear, our deep and loving friendship survived—even if our marriage did not.

Overcome Your Fears

Sometimes, in spite of a clear vision for the future, fear prevents our pursuit of a dream. Perhaps it is a fear of failure, or making a wrong decision. Perhaps it is fear of the unknown, or taking a risk. Speaking from experience, risk-taking in life and in business is unavoidable. In fact, there are just as many risks to standing still as there are from taking action.

Stepping upon a path is the first step to overcoming your fears as this simple activity often distracts the mind from becoming paralyzed by "what if."

Inviting others to join in your undertakings—your partner or a capable team—can help you analyze and negotiate difficult experiences. Know who your lifesavers are, share your vision with them, empower them, and they will be there to help you survive the tough business or personal landscapes you may encounter on your journey.

Let Go And Delegate!

The ancient Chinese symbol of Yin and Yang reminds us that there are opposites in everything and each of these opposites "produces" the other. There is no light without darkness, no joy without sorrow, no success without failure. The positive side of the leader personality is the ability to do what it takes to get things done; the negative side is the delusion that no one can do what needs to be done but them! In many cases, this delusion becomes a roadblock to a leader's own success when he or she obstructs a key employee's ability to access critical information, make decisions on his own, or lead a team or project in his own style. Recruiting a great team will not produce a victory if team members are never allowed into the game.

On the other hand, if a leader is brave enough to delegate responsibilities, unleash the natural talents of employees (especially when their talents and abilities are superior), and empower them with knowledge, tools, and the autonomy they need to manage their own success, victory is almost guaranteed.

So go ahead, let go and delegate. You might be surprised at how well your employees can run the business without you—and you might find yourself happily writing a book on a beach as a result!

Plan Ahead

As the leader, it is not only your responsibility to have a plan but to clearly communicate the plan to everyone on your team (and sometimes the outside world). Make sure everyone is working towards clearly defined goals—a higher degree of awareness will increase enthusiasm, passion and motivation.

Green Industry businesses are fortunate to have extended "downtime" in the winter months. Take advantage of this down time and use it to re-evaluate, refine, and improve your business from the inside out. Assemble your team to identify short- and long-term goals, revise your business plan, establish budgets for the new season, refine records, reports and operational procedures, assess existing personnel, equipment and vehicles and outline what's needed for the next year, and set new goals for all to aspire to.

The off-season is also great time to help existing employees enhance their skills and value to the company. Encourage them to attend workshops or classes to continue their educations and advance their careers.

Never Give Up!

What can I say about this last lesson? It is only by glancing back along the path I have traveled that enables me to advise people—with great enthusiasm and certainty—to never give up, in spite of setbacks and letdowns. For every step backward, be determined enough to take the next two steps forward and you will eventually reach your goals.

Don't get stuck in today's success. Move on with each new day. Continue to improve your business methods, operation procedures and communications. This keeps your business healthy and vibrant and alive—ready for any new trends that might require a shift in marketing strategies or business tactics. Everything worthwhile in life takes effort, persistence, and a drive to make it happen. Keep your eye on the future, use your sense of integrity and life's lessons as your road map, expect the landscape to have hills as well as valleys, draw energy from your friends and family as your fuel, and you will find the fortitude to push on with your dreams.

Lessons From The Landscape

Reflecting back on the path, it is clear to me now that I could only have accomplished what I have thus far with the love, support and continued camaraderie of my family, friends, and the many great employees and clients who have been involved with my business from its inception. It has been my goal to show my continued appreciation to those who have supported me through the years. Each one of them has been a critical component to my success. Needless to say, I am grateful to them all.

Beyond this, it also gives me great pleasure to appreciate people at random on a daily basis. Giving someone a compliment, extending an unexpected courtesy, sharing a smile with a stranger—such little niceties generate surprising results. Showing appreciation for people, and yourself, every day makes life very rewarding. I conclude with a quote from Ralph Waldo Emerson on the topic of success:

> "To laugh often and much; to win the respect of intelligent people and affection of children; to earn the appreciation of honest critics and endure the betrayal of false friends; to appreciate beauty, to find the best in others; to leave the world a bit better, whether by a healthy child, a garden patch, or a redeemed social condition; to know even one life has breathed easier because you have lived. This is to have succeeded."

I do not know where my journey will take me from here, but I will enjoy each precious moment, embrace change, appreciate people, and walk in integrity—because that is the only path I know.

BIBLIOGRAPHY

Leadership

Blanchard, Ken. 1999. The Heart of a Leader. Tulsa, Okla: Honor Books.

Blanchard, Ken. 2004. Leadership Smarts—Inspiration and Wisdom from the Heart of a Leader. Colorado Springs, Colo: Honor Books.

Blanchard, Ken. 2004. The On-Time, On-Target Manager: How "Last Minute Manager" Conquered Procrastination. New York: Harper Collins Publishers, Inc.

Blanchard, Ken, Bill Hybels, and Phil Hodges. 1999. Leadership by the Book: Tools to Transform Your Workplace. New York City: William Morrow and Company, Inc.

Blanchard, Ken, and Marc Muchnick. 2003. The Leadership Pill: The Missing Ingredient in Motivating People Today. New York City: Free Press.

Blanchard, Ken, Patricia Zigarmi, and Drea Zigarmi. 1985. Leadership and The One Minute Manager: Increasing Effectiveness Through Situational Leadership. New York City: William Morrow and Company, Inc.

Genett, Donna M. Ph.D. 2003. If You Want it Done Right, You Don't Have To Do It Yourself! The Power of Effective Delegation. Sanger, Calif: Quill Driver Books/Word Dancer Press, Inc.

Hayward, Steven F. 1997. Churchill on Leadership—Executive Success in the Face of Adversity. Rocklin, Calif: Prima Publishing.

Jennings, Ken and John Stahl-Wert. 2003. The Serving Leader—5 Powerful Actions That Will Transform Your Team, Your Business, and Your Community. San Francisco: Berrett-Koehler Publishers, Inc.

Manchester, William. 1983. The Last Lion: Winston Spencer Churchill; Visions of Glory: 1874-1932. Boston: Little, Brown and Company.

Manchester, William. 1988. The Last Lion: Winston Spencer Churchill; Alone: 1932-1940. Boston: Little, Brown and Company.

Maxwell, John C. 2002. Leadership 101. Nashville: Thomas Nelson Publishers.

Maxwell, John C. 2001. The 17 Indisputable Laws of Teamwork – Embrace Them and Empower Your Team. Nashville: Thomas Nelson Publishers.

Maxwell, John C. 1999. The 21 Indispensable Qualities of a Leader – Becoming the Person Others Will Want to Follow. Nashville: Thomas Nelson, Inc.

Sandys, Celia and Jonathan Littman. 2003. We Shall Not Fail – The Inspiring Leadership of Winston Churchill. London, England: Penguin Group.

Motivation:

Bauer, Joel and Mark Levy. 2004. How to Persuade People Who Don't Want to Be Persuaded: Get What You Want—Every Time! Hoboken, N.J.: John Wiley and Sons, Inc.

Blanchard, Kenneth and Sheldon Bowles. 1998. Gung Ho! New York City: William Morrow and Company, Inc.

Blanchard, Kenneth and Sheldon M. Bowles. 1993. Raving Fans – A Revolutionary Approach to Customer Service. New York City: William Morrow and Company, Inc.

Blanchard, Ken, Dana Robinson, and Jim Robinson. 2002. Zap the Gaps! Target Higher Performance and Achieve It! New York City: Harper Collins Publishers, Inc.

Bruce, Anne and James S. Pepitone. 1999. Motivating Employees. New York City: McGraw Hill.

Connellan, Thomas K. Ph.D. 2003. Bringing Out the Best in Others! Three Keys for Business Leaders, Educators, Coaches, and Parents. Austin, Texas: Bard Press.

Johnson, Spencer. M.D. 1998. Who Moved My Cheese? New York City, NY: G.P. Putnam's and Sons.

Mitchell, Jack. 2003. Hug Your Customers – The Proven Way to Personalize Sales and Achieve Outstanding Results. New York City: Hyperion.

Rye, David. 2002. Attracting and Rewarding Outstanding Employees. Newburgh, N.Y.: Entrepreneur Press.

Cappelli, Peter, adviser. 2002. Hiring and Keeping the Best People. Boston: Harvard Business School Press.

Success

Canfield, Jack, Mark Victor Hansen, and Les Hewitt. 2000. The Power of Focus. Deerfield Beach, Fla: Health Communications, Inc.

Carnegie, Dale. 1981. How To Win Friends and Influence People. New York City: Pocket Books.

Covey, Stephen R. 1999. Living the 7 Habits – Stories of Courage and Inspiration. New York City: Simon & Schuster.

DarConte, Lorraine A., ed. 2001. Lessons For Success. New York City:

Barnes & Noble Books.

Decker, Joe with Eric Neuhaus. 2004. The World's Fittest You. New York City: Dutton.

Gitomer, Jeffrey H. 1994. The Sales Bible. New York City: William Morrow and Company, Inc.

Lasher, William. 1994. The Perfect Business Plan Made Simple. New York City: Doubleday.

Levine, Stuart R. 2004. The Six Fundamentals of Success – The Rules for Getting It Right for Yourself and Your Organization. New York City: Currency Doubleday.

Lombardi, Vince Jr. 2005. The Lombardi Rules – 26 Lessons from Vince Lombardi: The World's Greatest Coach. New York City: McGraw Hill.

Michaelson, Gerald A. 2001. Sun Tzu- The Art of War for Managers—50 Strategic Rules. Avon, Ohio: Adams Media Corporation.

Michaelson, Gerald, with Steven Michaelson. 2003. Sun Tzu for Success – How to Use the Art of War to Master Challenges and Accomplish the Important Goals in Your Life. Avon, Ohio: Adams Media Corporation.

Maxwell, John C. 2000. Failing Forward – Turning Mistakes Into Stepping Stones for Success. Nashville: Nelson Books.

Sanborn, Mark. 2004. The Fred Factor – How Passion in Your Work and Life Can Turn the Ordinary into the Extraordinary. New York City, NY: Currency Doubleday.

Wellness

Carlson, Richard. Ph.D. 1998. Don't Sweat the Small Stuff at Work – Simple Ways to Minimize Stress and Conflict While Bringing Out the Best in Yourself and Others. New York City: Hyperion.

Carlson, Richard. Ph.D. 2005. Easier Than You Think ... because life doesn't have to be so hard! New York City: Harper San Francisco.

Johnson, Spencer. M.D. 2003. The Present – The Gift That Makes You Happier and More Successful at Work and in Life, Today! New York City: Doubleday.

Kabat-Zinn, Jon. 1994. Wherever You Go, There You Are—Mindfulness Meditation in Everyday Life. New York City: Hyperion.

Real, Terrence. 1997. I Don't Want to Talk About It – Over-coming the Secret Legacy of Male Depression. New York City: Scribner.

Tolle, Eckhart. 1999. The Power of Now – A Guide to Spiritual Enlightenment. Novato, Calif: Namaste Publishing and New World Library.

Ryan, M. J. 1999. Attitudes of Gratitude – How to Give and Receive Joy Every Day of Your Life. New York City: Barnes & Noble Books.

Ruiz, Don Miguel. 2000. The Four Agreements Companion Book. San Rafael, Calif: Amber-Allen Publishing.

Stoddard, Alexandra. 1990. Daring to Be Yourself. New York City: Quill/Harper Collins.

Book Order Form

Please send me _____ copies of "Lessons From the Landscape" for $19.95 per copy (U.S.) plus $4.95 to cover shipping and handling.

Name _____
Company _____
Street Address _____
City, State, Zip _____
E-mail Address _____
Telephone: _____

Payment Information

Total Due:

If paying with a check or money order, please make payable to: Frank Crandall.

If paying with Master Card or Visa, please provide required information below:

Card Type: [ ] Master Card   [ ] Visa
Card Number: _____
Expiration Date: _____

Cardholder Signature: _____

[ ] Please autograph this book.
[ ] Please sign this gift to _____

Order forms for this book available at www.woodriverevergreens.com

WOOD RIVER PRODUCTIONS
101 Woodville Road, Hope Valley, RI 02832 - 401-364-3387